DECODABLE READER

24544

READ
Srilfdr
2016

www.*FLEX*Literacy.com

Send all inquiries to:
McGraw-Hill Education
8787 Orion Place
Columbus, OH 43240

ISBN: 978-0-02-140095-9
MHID: 0-02-140095-4

Printed in the United States of America.

5 6 7 8 9 10 QVS 20 19 18 17 16

Contents

Contents

Sam

Sam sat at mat.
"Sam! Sam! Sam! Sam!"

Matt sat at mat.
"Matt! Matt! Matt! Matt!"

"Sam! Matt! Sam! Matt! Sam! Matt!"

Matt sat. Sam sat.

Teacher: *The wrestling match continues. The wrestlers try their hardest while the crowd cheers them on. Who will win the match?*

Matt

Matt sat at mat.
"Matt! Matt! Matt! Matt!"

Sam sat at mat.
"Sam! Sam! Sam! Sam!"

Matt sat. Sam sat.
"Sam! Matt! Sam! Matt! Sam! Matt!"

Sass?

Dad sat.

Sam? Matt?
Sam, Matt, Dad sat.

Tad? Tam?
Tad, Tam, Matt, Sam, Dad sat.

Sad Sass.
Sass?
Sass, Tam, Tad, Matt, Sam, Dad sat.

Dad at Dam

Dad sat.

Dad sat at mat.

Dad sat at dam.

At dam, Dad sat at mat.

Teacher: *Tam's and Ed's neighbors moved away. Tam is sad. Ed is angry. They miss their friends. Then, sad Tam and mad Ed see a moving van. A car with three kids arrives. Tam and Ed run to meet their new neighbors—Ted, Tess, and Sam.*

Sad Tam, Mad Ed

Sad Tam sat.
Mad Ed sat.

Sad Tam met Ted. She met Tess.
She met Sam.
Tam met Ted, Tess, Sam!

Mad Ed met Ted. He met Tess.
He met Sam.
Ed met Ted, Tess, Sam!

Teacher: Beavers chew trees and use the logs from fallen trees to build homes, or lodges, and dams around their lodges. A beaver dam is a mass of sticks, rocks, and mud that can look like a mess! Ted is looking at a beaver dam.

Mess?

Mess! Ted sat.

Mess? Mass? Ted sat.

Ted sat at mess?
He sat at mass!

Ted sat at dam.

Teacher: Tad's Fast Food makes its food really fast. Tad and his waitstaff give food to their customers fast. Is it too fast? Will the customers enjoy their fast food?

Fast Tad

Matt sat at Tad's.
Tad fed Matt fast!
He fed Matt a sad mess.

Sam sat at Tad's.
Tad's staff fed Sam fast!
He fed Sam a sad mess.

Tad's fed Matt, Sam fast!

Teacher: *Tess learned in science class that celery is the stem of a plant. She also learned that rabbits can eat celery. At home, Tess has three rabbits—Ted, Tam, and Tad—that like to eat vegetables. Tess decides to feed them some celery stems.*

Tess Fed Stems

Tess sat.

Ted sat, Tam sat, Tad sat!

Tess fed Ted stems.
She fed Tam stems.
She fed Tad stems.

She fed Ted, Tam, Tad!

Teacher: *Ted has a cat named Stef. Ted puts a small camera around Stef's neck. This neck cam will record everything Stef does and everything Ted does!*

Stef's Cam

Ted set Stef's cam.
Stef's cam?
Cat cam!

Ted sat. Stef sat.
Cat cam sat.

Stef acts sad.
Cat cam acts sad.

Ted fed Stef at Stef's cam!

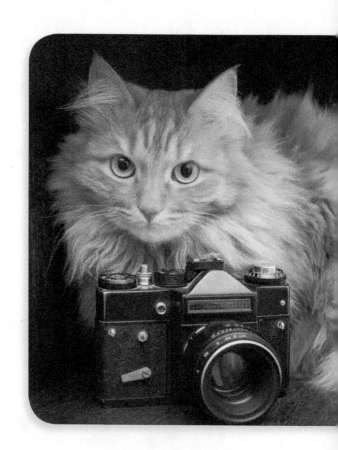

Cat Facts

Cat facts!

Fact: At mat, cat sat.
Fact: She acts sad.
Fact: Cat fed.
Fact: Fast cat!

The Mitt

The mitt is stiff.
Did it fit Mac?
It did fit!
The mitt fits Mac.

Mac's fist fit the mitt.

Dad sat.

"Did the mitt fit, Mac?"

"It did, Dad."

Sad Mac's fist fit the mitt.

Teacher: *Miss Stam has a circus dog act. Cass and Tess are two dogs in the act. Ted has a dog named Sid. Ted trained Sid for Miss Stam's dog act. Now Ted watches Miss Stam test how well Sid is trained. Can Sid be part of the act?*

Miss Stam's Act

It is the Cass, Tess, Sid act!

"Sit at the mat, Cass."
Cass did. Cass sat at Miss Stam's mat.

"Sit at the mat, Tess."
Tess did. Tess sat at Miss Stam's mat.

"Sit at the mat, Sid."
Did Sid? He sat at Ted!

It is the Cass, Tess Act!

Red Raft

At the raft, Fred sits.
The red raft sits. Fast?
Fred sits.

The raft rests at the dam.
Fred rests at the dam.

Red, red, red Fred rests.
Fred, the red mess, rests!

Teacher: *Years ago, huge trees were cut down, and the logs were tied together to make giant rafts. Brave men floated the rafts down the Mississippi River. The logs were sold to use in constructing houses and buildings.*

Dim Mist

Dim mist.

The raft sits, sits.

We add the mast.

The raft is fast, fast, fast!

Raft is at the dam!

At the dam, we rest.

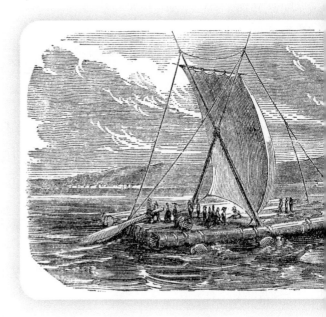

15

A Hat? A Dress?

Steff sat. Steff had a red hat.

The red hat had a ram. Did the hat fit? Did it fit Steff? Steff!

She had Matt's red hat.

Matt sat. Matt had a red dress!

It had a red, red hem. It had red, red trim. Did it fit Matt? Did it fit him? Matt!

He had Steff's red dress!

Hiss!

Tess the cat sits. Tess rests at the red mat.

Dad has Taft the cat. Dad sets him at the red mat.

Dad sits at the red mat. Did Taft sit?

Tess acts mad! Hiss! Hiss! Hiss!

Did Taft sit? Sad Taft acts fast! He hid!

Tess sits. She rests at the red mat.

Teacher: Dad has two cameras that can be attached to rafts. The cameras are different sizes. The cameras take pictures. Dad calls pictures "pics."

Cams and Rafts

Dad sets a cam at Matt's raft. Dad tests Matt's cam. "That cam fits this raft, Matt."

Dad sets a cam at Steff's raft. Dad tests Steff's cam. "That cam fits this raft, Steff."

Matt and Steff sit. Matt's raft hits Steff's! Steff's raft hits Matt's! The rafts hit fast!

Matt's cam had Steff's raft. Steff's cam had Matt's raft.

Mist

A mass hits *Mist!* That mass rams it. It rams Tam and Matt. This mass hits the cam. The cam!

Act fast, Tam! That cam is fast! Tam did act fast.

Tam did it! Tam had the cam.
Tam sets the cam at *Mist.* Tam hits the cam.
That did it! The cam fits to *Mist.*

Matt tests the cam. Tam rests.

Teacher: Tom Taft likes to put red dots on things. He uses paint, pencils, and markers.

Red Dots!

Tom Taft had a hat. It had red dots.

Tom Taft had a cot. It had red dots.

Tom Taft had a raft. That raft had a mass of red dots.

Tom Taft had a fast hot rod. It had red trim and red dots!

Tom Taft had a mom. Mom Taft's dress had red dots.

Tom Taft had a cat. It hid!

Teacher: At Sunken Mast Lake, there is an old fish called Odd Todd. People have tried to catch Odd Todd for years. But Odd Todd is too smart to be caught. Today, the Smith family has Dot's lucky fishing rod. Is this the day that Odd Todd gets caught?

Odd Todd

Tam had Dot's rod. She had it at this red raft. Did she miss Odd Todd? She did.

Tom had Dot's rod. He sat at that mast. He did miss Odd Todd.

Mom had Dot's rod. She sat and sat. She did miss Odd Todd.

Dad had Dot's rod. Dad sat at the red raft. Odd Todd hid. Did Dad miss Odd Todd? Dad did!

And Odd Todd had Dot's rod!

Can Nan?

Nat can stand on a hand. Can Nan?

Fran can mend a dress. Can Nan?

Mom can sand a raft. Can Nan?

Dad can fit a cam to a hat. Can Nan?

Nan can fit a cam to a hat, sand a raft, mend a dress, and stand on a hand!

Can Dad? Can Mom? Can Fran? Can Nat?

Ants and Ham

A tin can sits in hot, hot sand.
An ant sits in the sand.

That ant ran to the tin can.
Ham! A fact. A can of ham!

That ant ran to the ant nest.
That ant did not rest. Ants
and ants ran to the tin can in
the sand. The ants had ham!

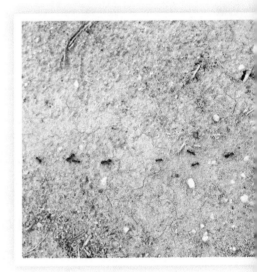

Teacher: Band practice is about to start. Biff, the brass band director, is standing at his music stand. The band members are not quite ready to start. Most are walking around and chatting. Biff tells them to sit.

Sit!

Biff is at the stand. "In a bit, sit. Sit. Sit."

The brass band did not sit. Bob, Nan, and the rest of the band did not sit.

"Sit! Sit!! Bob, Nan, and the rest of you, sit!"

A bit of the band sat. Bob, Nan, and the rest of the band did not sit.

Biff's hand hit the stand! BAM! BAM! BAM! "SIT! SIT! SIT!"

That brass band sat!

Teacher: *The Sahara desert in Africa has some strange animals. The sand cat is cute, but it is fast and dangerous. The fat sand rat looks like a gerbil. When a sand cat hunts for fat sand rats, watch out!*

Fast!

A sand cat hid. A sand cat is a bit tan and a bit red. Tan and red hid it in sand.

Is that a fat sand rat? The sand cat bent a bit. It is!

The sand cat acts fast! It ran fast! Bam! It hits the fat sand rat. Bam! It bats that fat sand rat. It hits and bats that fat sand rat. Bam! Bam! Bam!

Socks?

Rick is on the bed. Tick. Tick. Tick. Rick cannot rest. Rick did miss Socks, the cat.

Hiss! Hiss! Ricks stands. "Is that a hiss at the deck?"

Hiss! Hiss! "Is that you, Socks? Is Socks on the deck? Is Socks back?"

In a bit, Rick is at the deck. "Is Socks on this deck?"

Socks is not! Mist is on the deck. A cat sat in that mist!

Did sad Rick miss Socks?

Teacher: The good news is that no one was hurt. The bad news is that an earthquake caused serious damage. This is what one witness said.

Rocks Hit Fast!

It hit at ten. It did not end fast.

Rocks hit the deck in back. Rocks hit this dock. The dock did not stand. A bit of the dock sits in the sand.

Rocks hit a cab. Rocks bent the cab!

Rocks hit the bandstand! A rock hit the tent. We hid.

It is bad! It is a mess.

A Wet West Wind

Steff ran in a wet west wind. She ran fast. Wet mist and swift wind hit Steff.

In back of Steff, Mack ran. Mack ran fast in back. The wet west wind hit Steff. That wet wind did not hit him.

Can Steff win? Can Mack win? The wet west wind hit Steff. And a bit of wind hit Mack. Steff can win in a wet west wind!

Teacher: *Mick and Mack are friends. They have spent their whole lives together. But now Mick lives in the western part of the United States. Mack lives in the eastern part. They use computers and cell phones to see each other on the Web.*

Mick and Mack on the Web

Mick is in the west. Mack is not.

On the Web, Mick sat in the hot sand. Mack did not.

On the Web, Mack ran fast as the wind. Mick did not.

On the Web, Mick had a raft. Mack did not.

On the Web, Mack did a handstand. Mick did not.

On the Web, Mick did not miss Mack. Mack did not miss Mick.

29

Teacher: In a restaurant kitchen, a man is stacking dishes on a rack.
What could possibly go wrong?

A Dish Stack

A dish stack sits on a rack. The stack is red dish, tan dish, red dish, tan dish, on and on.

I stand. I set a tan dish on that stack.
I wish I had not!

I stand back. That stack did not stand. I stand back!

That stack went fast!

Crash! Smash! Smash! Crash!

That dish stack was a stack. It is a mess of red and tan dish bits!

A Shock!

Red ants wish not to be wet. That is not a shock.

This is a shock. If a nest is wet, red ants band in a mass. Red ants stick to red ants! That mass is a red ant raft! That is a shock!

Fish can get red ants. The raft can crash, smash on rocks.

That red ant raft can pass to a fresh nest.

Teacher: *Tish and Mick want to raft to the rock. Why doesn't Ben?*

Not Me!

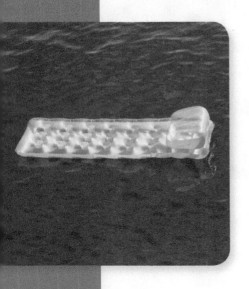

Tish and I sat on Red Fish Dock.

"We can raft to that rock. We can fish at that rock!" she said.

"Not me," I said.

Mick sat on the dock.

"We can raft to that rock. It can be fast!" he said.

"Not me," I said.

"Tish and I can. You can, Ben!" he said.

"You can, Ben!" said Tish.

"Not me. I am not a fish fan!" I said.

Teacher: *Mack and his twin sister Beck are planning to make a cartoon movie about a superhero. They just cannot decide what the superhero will be like.*

Mack and Beck!

"It can be a cat. It can smash with its fists," said Beck.

"He can be Mack, the Cat Man!" said Mack. "He can smash rocks! Bam!"

"Mack, the Cat Man?" said Beck. "She can be Beck, the Fast Cat! She can be fast!"

"Mack!" said Mack.

"Beck!" said Beck.

"Can it be Mack and Beck? Mack can smash," said Mack.

"And Beck is fast," said Beck.

Mack and Beck, the Cats!

A "G" Hat

The big grab bag was on the stand. The bag was big and fat. You stick a hand in and grab.

I got to stick a hand in that bag. I got a hat. It had a "G" on it. It was a Grand Band hat. That is a rock band. I am a fan!

A "G" hat can be a grand dad hat. Get it?

I hand that hat to Grand Dad. He got it!

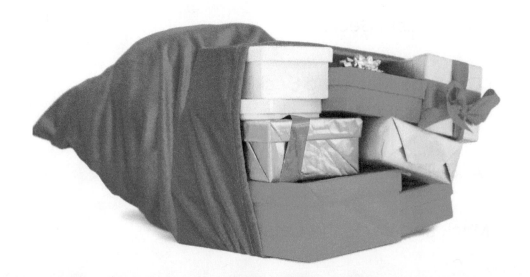

Teacher: Scientists track frogs to learn how and where frogs live. Scientists put bands on frogs' legs. The bands are tags that identify the frog and track it. Some tags send information electronically to scientists. Grant is a scientist who studies frogs.

Grant and the Frog

Can Grant grab a frog in a net?

A frog sits on a wet rock. Grant gets it. That was fast! Grant sets the frog in a frog bag.

Back at a tent, Grant sets a band on the frog. This band is a tag that can track the frog. The tag can send frog facts to Grant.

Grant is back at that wet rock. He sets the frog back on the rock.

Teacher: *Mom is in a hurry to leave. Dad sets out a bag of snacks for Mom to take with her. What do you think happens to the snacks?*

Snacks in a Bag

It was ten! Mom had to go fast. She had to get gas. She had to get Bo, the dog, to Doc Taft's.

Dad set snacks in a bag. "Grab that bag. Snacks are in it," said Dad to Mom.

Mom had to go, go, go!

Mom did not grab the bag. It sat.

"Did Mom grab that bag? No!" Dad said to Nan, the cat.

"Snacks are in that bag.
Did she grab the snacks?
No!" said Dad.

"So we can grab the snacks!"
said Dad. Nan and Dad had
the snacks.

Fast?

Are you as fast as a cat or a dog? If you and a cat go fast to its dish or its bed, can you win? No!

If you and that cat go fast to a stack of rocks and back, can the cat win? No. A cat cannot go fast on and on. So you can win.

If you and a dog dash to a stack of rocks, can you win? No!

If you and that dog go fast on and on, can the dog win? No, a dog cannot go fast on and on.

Teacher: *It is raining at the camp, and Pat and Peg are not happy. They want to raft on the pond or sit on the warm sand. What do you think happens?*

Damp Camp

The camp was a damp mess.

Pat sat in a tent. She had a camp map. "We cannot raft or sit on the sand. And the map is wet!" said mad Pat.

"I can nap," said sad Peg. "I cannot go sit at the pond."

"Stop!" said Pat. "We can go!" The camp was not wet!

"Tom is at the pond," said Peg.

"We can raft!" said Pat. Peg and Pat had to grin.

A Pest Pig

Can a pig be a pest? The pig in a pen is not a pest. A pig that is not in a pen can be a pest, a bad pest!

A pest pig can be big and fast. It can dig. It can grab frog eggs in a nest or grass or stems.

A pest pig can get fish at a pond. It can grab a dog, a cat, or rat. It can pick a bat!

A pest pig can smash a pen. It can grab a pen pig!

Fern

Fern ran a big brass band.
Her band was Fern and the Brass Pack.

Fern was at her stand. The band sat.

Fern was stern as she ran her band. Fern hit her stand. "Tap! Tap! Tap!"

Her band hit back at her. "Tap! Tap! Tap!"

Stern Fern hit her stand. "Rap! Rap! Rap!"

Her band hit back at her. "Rap! Rap! Rap!"

Mad Fern hit her stand. "Bam! Bam! Bam!"

Her band hit back at her. "Bam! Bam! Bam!"

Stern Fern had to grin a bit. The band had to grin a bit back at her.

A Ship

Sherm and Fern are on a ship. Sherm and Fern stand at a mast in the aft of the ship. "Aft is a ship term. Aft is in a ship's back," said Sherm.

"And the back back end is the stern. Stern is a ship term," said Fern.

At the stern, Fern had to grab her hat. Wind hit it. It was damp on the stern of the ship. Wet mist hit Sherm and Fern.

Sherm said, "That is a herd of fish!"

"Herd is not the term, Sherm!" said Fern. Fern and Sherm grin.

Bump

Bud and his dog Bump ran at the pond. Bud had a stick.

Bud said, "Can you run and get the stick, Bump?"

Bud sent that stick up, up, up! Did Bump run to get it? Bump did run, but not so fast.

Bump ran for a bit in the mud. Bump had to stop at a bug on a fern. He had to stop at a nut stuck in wet mush. Bump had to rest in the sun.

Bump did get the stick. But Bud had to nap. So Bump set the stick on Bud.

Bats!

Duck! A Bat!

If it is a bat, we run. We are not bat fans. Bats are not fun!

But bats are not bad. As you rest in bed, bats hunt bug pests. As you rest, they get rid of a big, big mass of bug pests! The bug pests that bats hunt are bad for us.

If the sun is up, bats rest. Cats can hunt for bats at rest. If a cat gets a bat, it can be bad for us. Can cats get rid of bug pests? Cats cannot!
Bats can!

A Whiff!

When Dad can, he whips up stuff for a bun. It can be ham or egg on a bun. He whips up this bun stuff on a whim. So he grabs this and that for the bun.

Ham or egg on a bun is not bad. But his fish, nuts, egg, and mint mess is bad! Bad!

When Dad whips up his stuff for a bun, I stand in back and get a whiff. When that whiff is not bad, I step in and sit. When I get a bad whiff, I run fast! Fast!

Duck Nest

A duck is at a pond. She hunts in the grass for a bit of a dip. When she picks a dip, she sets up a nest.

Grass hid the nest, the dip, and the duck. When the wind whips fast, it cannot hit the nest. But the duck can get a whiff of pond mist.

Men mend a dock at the pond. As they hit and whack the dock, the duck sits in the nest. The men cannot see the duck.

The duck rests. When she gets an egg, it can be in this nest.

Bill

Bill slid on a hat and ran in the wind. With his hat on, he did not see Sal or the bell in her hand. He did not see her red pot.

He did not see me slip cash in that pot. That cash will help ill pets.

With his hat on, Bill ran at Sal!

Sal, the bell, and the pot fell! As Sal fell, Bill and I got her. We had to pick up the bell, pot, and a bit of cash.

Bill felt bad. But he did fill the pot with his cash! Sal was glad.

Sled Hill

In the past, this big hill was a trash dump. It had a bad smell. It was not fun to go past.

But when the dump was shut, the dump men had a plan. It was to set lots of land on top of the dump. On that hill, the plan was to plant grass. That dump was to be a sled hill.

The men did set land on that dump. They did plant grass. They did set up a sled hill!

The sled hill is not fun to pass up. It is fun to stop and sled!

Chet's Bench

Chet had a bench for his deck. But the bench did not fit. It was a bit big.

"I will cut this bench, but not by much. I will cut it an inch or so. It will fit," said Chet.

Chet cut an inch, but his bench did not fit. "I still have to cut an inch," he said.

Chet did. That bench still did not fit! Chet said, "I will chop an inch or so."

Chet did chop, chop, and chop.

Did Chet chop the bench to bits? He did! Chet had to sit on the deck!

Cats

If you have a pet cat, it gets a bed. You check that it is well and fed.

If you see a cat in the grass or in rocks, is it a pet? Was it glad to see you, or did it hiss at you? Which is it? If it did hiss, it is not a pet.

Such a cat cannot be fed by you. Such a cat will hunt as much as it can. Such a cat will not have a bed. You cannot pet such a cat. It is not a pet!

Chet and Ann

Chet and Ann were at Chet's hot grill. "Will you test a snack?" said Chet.

"A snack? Yes!" said Ann.

"It will have mint," said Chet.

"Yum! Yum! I am a big mint fan!" said Ann.

"It will have a bit of dill!" said Chet.

"Yum! Yum! I am a dill fan!" said Ann.

"I will hand the snack to you," said Chet.

Ann had a bit of Chet's snack.

"Yuck! Is this yam? Did you grill yam?" said Ann.

"Yes," said Chet.

"Yuck! Yuck! I am not a yam fan!" said Ann.

Chet and Ann grin.

Yam Fests!

Dad sat by Mom. He had a map. Dad was a yam fan. In fact, he was a Yam Fest fan!

"Can you pick a Yam Fest yet?" said Mom.

Mom was not as big a yam fan as Dad.

"Yes! We can go to ten," said Dad.

"Ten?" said Mom.

"Yep! Ten!" said Dad with a yell.

"Or we can go to the best Yam Fest," said Mom.

"Yes, we can go to the best Yam Fest!" said Dad.

Mom was glad.

"Then we can go to the rest!" he said.

Mom was sad.

"Yum!" said Dad.

A Run

Beth ran. She had on a thin top and pants. She did not run in thick stuff. On her run, that thick stuff got hot!

Beth ran up the path. The sun was not up yet. In this tenth of the run, Beth felt wind and chill. She ran past the band shell.

Past the band shell, the chill had left. The sun was up. Fast men ran on the path. Beth ran past them.

By the end of her run, Beth was hot. Her thin top and pants were hot. She had run well.

Math

Math can help.

You have to mend a deck. You must cut a log for that deck. Will it fit? Math can tell you. Cut that log by an inch!

You set a big rack on a rug. The rack tips a bit to the left. Can a thick or thin pad on the left stop that tip? Math can help. Yes. Stick in a pad that is a tenth of an inch thick.

You must hem a dress so it will fit. Math can help! Math can tell you to hem it an inch.

Yes, math can help!

A Camp Kit

Kim and Mom sat in their den. Kim had a tan camp kit. It had one cup and a dish. "What is this?" said Kim.

"It is Gramps's camp kit," said Mom.

"Was Gramps a kid then?" said Kim.

"No, he was a man," said Mom.

"Were you a kid then?" said Kim.

"Not yet," said Mom, with a grin.

Then Mom said, "I miss him."

Mom and Kim felt sad.

Then Kim said, "Can I sip with Gramps's camp cup?"

Mom had to kiss Kim.

"Yes, Kim, you can!" said Mom.

Plants That Kill

Can a bug kill a plant? Yes.

Can a plant kill a bug? Not a lot of plants can kill a bug. But still, plants can kill a bug.

One plant that can kill will have a trap. The trap can snap shut on a bug. The bug will be kept in that trap!

Or a bug will stick to a plant. The bug can kick and kick, but it will still be kept on that plant.

Shops sell kits of plants that can kill bug pests. Shops can tell you what plants kill a bug.

Mud

"Let's run in the Mud Jog!" said Jess.

"That will get mud on us! We will have fun!" said Jan.

On the Mud Jog path, Jan slips in mud. Jess did not slip.

Jess jumps past one mud pit. Jan just jumps in it.

Jess jumps past a net. Jan slips at the net. She hits the mud.

Jess and Jan jig and jog on the path. Jan slips and dips in mud.

At the end of their run, much mud is on Jan. But no mud is on Jess!

"I got the mud! I win!" said Jan.

Jet Pack

The man will test a jet pack. That is his job.

Will he grab a pack and get on a jet? No, he will not. His pack is on his back. Jets are in that pack. The jets run on gas. The jets will send the man up!

The man will not have to jump up. He just lets the jet pack lift him. He will not jump or hop.

With this jet pack, the man can jig and jog past this spot. He can land at that one. He will be back fast.

Red Fuzz

Buzz and I sit at a path. We spot a man run. He is fast! A whiz!

The man runs with a red fuzz hat on. As he zips past, red fuzz bits land on us.

In a bit, the man zips back. His hat is still on. He spots red fuzz on us. He stops. "Did you see a red fuzz hat? Did it drop?"

I stand up and grab his hat. "Is this the one?"

"Yes! I am glad you have it."

With his hat back on, the man ran. Buzz and I just grin!

Buzz!

A bug zips at you. Buzz! What facts
can that buzz tell you? It can tell you
that a bug is by you. It can tell you
that you can get bit. It can tell you to
wag a hand so that bug will whiz past.
That buzz can tell you a lot!

But a bug will not buzz to tell you
facts. What can that buzz tell a bug?

One bug will buzz to get a bug pal.
That buzz can send bug facts. A bug
will buzz to tell bug facts to that pal,
not to you!

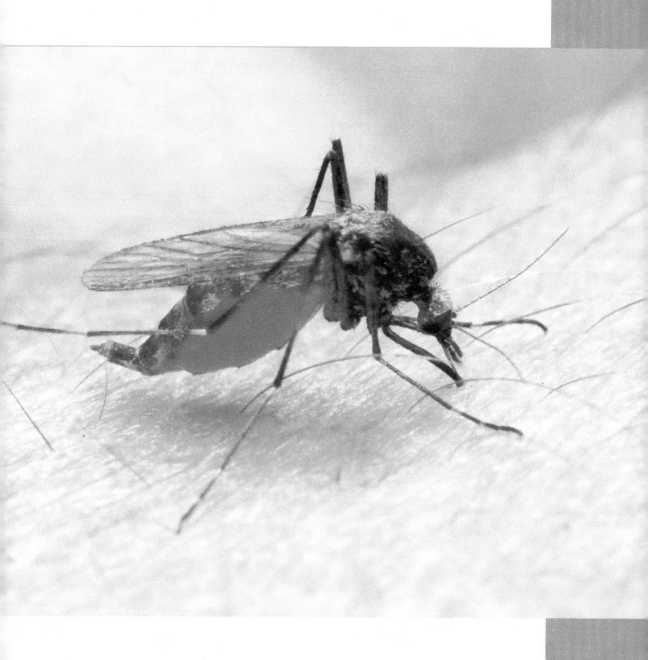

Flat or Fat?

Mike and Kath plan a bike ride. "Would you like to ride on the mud path?" said Mike.

"Yes, I have a fat tire bike," said Kath.

"A flat tire bike!" said Mike.

"No, a fat tire bike. A fat tire is wide and thick. It is best for wet mud."

On the path, Mike slides a bit on the mud. Kath bikes fast past Mike.

In time, Mike is by Kath. She sits on the side of the path. She is sad.

"I hit a rock," she said. "So I do have a flat tire bike!"

Do you like slime? You would like a slug.

A slug is a bit like a clam. A clam will have a shell and hide in wet spots like a pond.

A slug will not have a shell. It will hide on land. You can see a slug on the side of a deck or in grass. A slug will not like sun.

Slime is in a slug and on its skin. A slug can slide on its slime. If a frog bites a slug, it will not like the slime! Yuck! The frog will not like the slug.

Late for the Game

Mom was late. Her plane was late. She would miss Kate's game. Kate's game was by the spot that the plane would land. But Mom would still miss the game. The plane would not land on time. That would make Kate sad.

Mom had a plan. What would she do? Mom sat on the left side of the plane. When it was time for the plane to land, Mom had a cam. The plane tips a bit to its left. Mom can see Kate's game! Snap! Snap! Snap!

Mom had shots of Kate's game! Kate would be glad.

Snakes

Do you spot snakes in your grass or at your gate?
Do you spot them when you rake or cut grass?

Snakes hide well. They can hide in grass and rocks.
When it is hot, snakes rest in shade.

Do not hate snakes! Do not kill them. Snakes get
rid of pests. The same pests can make us sick. So
snakes can make us safe.

But a snake you spot is not your pal. Snakes do
bite. Be safe. Do not pick up snakes! Do not make a
snake mad!

Code?

Dad and I rode bikes at Stone Hill. We did not plan to ride up it.

Then smoke came up in back of Stone Hill. Smoke came up in big puffs and not-so-big puffs. Was this code? Was it a note? We had to see!

We rode up Stone Hill. On top, we did see smoke but no code. But we did get to see Stone Lake. The sun lit it up. It was the best! Still I said, "Was that smoke code? Nope!"

"It was!" Dad said. "It said 'Go see Stone Lake!'"

I am glad we did.

A Globe

A globe can sit on your desk. On a globe, can you see the USA? Yes, you can.

Can you see your home state? If that globe is big, you can.

Can you see your home? Nope!

On a globe, which pole is at the top? Name the pole that is not.

Can you spot Rome or Nome on the globe? Rome is not close to Nome!

Have you made trips to spots on this globe? Which spots? Name spots that you hope to go see.

Spin the globe and pick a fresh spot!

Gus

Gus sits at his desk. It is the shape of a cube. It is not big, but Gus is. He is a big dude! He just fits in at his desk.

On his desk, Gus has tape, pens, notes, and pads. He has a cute mug June sent him. He has a globe, lamp, and files. He has a flute case and a flute he must tune. His desk is a mess!

A bell chimes. Who is that? Big Gus gets up fast. His hips hit his desk. It tips! Can Gus stop it? It is no use. Crash!

Gus checks his desk. It is not the mess it had been. That is swell! But the rug is a mess! That is not swell.

Mule Trips

Who has been on a mule trip? I was last June!

In the West, mule trips are on cliff paths or slopes. A mule trip will take you to spots you will not get to if you just hike. You will see so much!

On a trip, you ride in a line. You are led by a pro who has much skill. He or she will help in your use of a mule.

When I rode on a trip, I had a big mule. His name was Dude.

Dude was cute and safe. If the path had risks, Dude would stop. Was that rude? It was not. "Be safe" is a mule rule.

So take a mule trip! It is fun.

My new van is not very new. It was Vick's. I gave him cash for it.

I set stuff in my new van. I set in a big stone vase and five big, flat rocks. I set in stuff to cut and trim grass.

Then I drive to the grove. I drive just a bit when my van stops! This new van will not go!

Are the tires flat? No. Did that stuff I set in this van make it stop? No. Is Vick's van just bad? I bet it is bad!

I am very mad! I check with Vick. Did he sell me a bad van?

"Dave, did you fill that van with gas?" Vick asks me.

I did not!

Cave Life

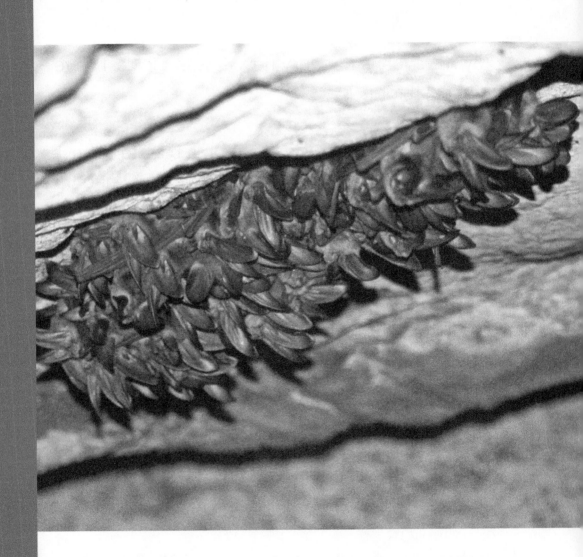

A thick vine can hide a cave. That cave can hide much life.

Bats rest in a cave. But bats hunt. In a grove or grass, they dip and dive to dine on pests. When the sun is up at five, bats go back to the cave.

A cave can be home to snakes. A thick snake will slide past the thick vine.

A cave can be home to very odd fish. They do not see! They dive in cave lakes and dine on bugs. A fish like this will spend its life in the cave.

A cave can be home to a bug that cannot see. It will dine on bits of skin. It can bite live skin!

Fox Lake

A big wind hits Fox Lake. It rips up a log dock!
When the wind stops, much of the dock sits in
Fox Lake.

I grab my fix-it box. I get six big men. We will fix the
dock. Max asks me, "Beth, can I cut up a fresh log
stack?"

I tell Max yes. While he chops with his ax, the rest
of us wade in the lake where the big log bits are.

These big log bits we may save. The rest we stick
in a box. We do not mix big and bad bits.

At six, we rest. We make a fire with bad log bits.
We fix a snack. When the sun is up, we can fix
the dock.

Red Fox

A red fox may be red or black. It can have a mix of white on it.

The den of a red fox can be very close to where you are. But you will not see it.

Fox cubs hide in the den. A fox can have five or six new pups.

A red fox can hunt and kill a vole, a rat, or a cat or dog. It can dine on these or on snacks you save for pets. It will snack on trash in a bag or box. Fix the lid on your trash so a fox will not get in!

A red fox can make a pet or you sick. Do not pet a fox!

Read! Read! Read!

When you sleep, the sun peeks up in the east. End your dream! Get up! Eat!

While you eat, read if you can! Read what you can! Read where you can!

What you read can tell if it will be hot or wet. You may need a hat and thick socks.

While you read, see if your team had a big game. Did they win it?

What you read will teach you which treat to eat. Which is best—a sweet peach, green grapes, or a wheat bun?

What you read can make you smile and grin a lot. Tell jokes that you read.

So read these tips. Sleep! Dream! Eat! Grin! Read!

A Beach

At the sea, a beach can teach you so much! Hike on a beach and take notes.

Is this beach just sand? Or do you see bits of stone or rocks? Are these green, red, tan, white, or black? Will a wave reach up and take them?

Is this beach clean and neat? Is it a mess?

What life do you see at this beach? Can you spot a shell? Where is it? Can you see a clam or a sand crab? Do you see a hole in the sand? What can sleep and eat in it? Can you spot a sea gull? If you have luck, you may see a seal!

Keep these notes. They will be fun to read at home.

Drive!

When I was a kid on a farm, Dad let me drive his car. I did not go far or fast. I made short trips in the yard by the barn.

One time at the farm, Dad got sick. It was bad! He had to get to Doc Parks fast. Dad made me drive!

That drive was so hard. I had to drive far to get where Doc Parks was. We made it! In a week, Dad was fine.

Then a man came to the farm. He had a star on his car and chest.

"Bart, I am glad you got your dad to Doc Parks," he said to me. "But that will be your last car drive as a kid."

And it was.

Farm Park

This park was a farm. It was my home when I was a kid.

See that dark red barn. When this was a farm, we would store corn and crops in it. But in the park, that barn is a spot to meet. It has a store. You can get art, plants, and more.

Grab a park map in the barn and then hike. A hike starts at that plant cart. That is where the hen yard was. It was a chore to feed chicks!

Your hike may be short. But if you go far, you will see land that had corn and beans.

It was smart to make my farm a park. I miss the farm, but I like this park.

At Bat

It was Pat's turn to bat. This game was close. The Sharks led the Jets by only two to one. Pat was a Jet. If she did not get a hit, this game would end.

"You can do it, Pat!" said her team. But the Jets were not sure. Pat did not hit well.

Then, bam! Pat got a long hit. She ran fast to first base. The Sharks still had to chase her hit. In a flash, she was past third!

Pat made a dash to home. She slid in the dirt. Was she safe? No! Pat was not. The Jets did not win.

It hurt not to win. But each girl on the Jets said, "You did your best, Pat."

White Shark

A white shark eats and eats. It can swim and turn fast. In a burst of speed, it can grab what it likes. The sea will churn and stir while the white shark has its meal. That will not take long.

Will a white shark hurt us? It will not plan on it. But can a shark tell if it spots a seal or only a man? It may take a bite or two just to check. It may not take a third bite, but the first bite can kill!

Do not swim, dive, or surf at dusk. Do not surf or dive in a dark shirt.

If you see a shark, do not flirt with it. Get to the beach!

Cents

"One cent is not much," said Jeff.

Jess made a face and said, "Nope."

"Yet my plan now is to save each cent I get. I drop each in a jar," Jeff said.

Jeff set down a big glass jar on his desk. "This is what I have since June," he said.

"Yikes! It did not take long to fill that jar!" said Jess.

"Also, I did spend cents to fix the fence, get feed for my pet mice, and to shop in the city."

"Nice!" said Jess. Then she stuck her hand in her shirt. She had two cents.

"Will you drop them in my jar?" said Jeff.

"Nope! I will drop these in a box at home," said Jess. "I will save cents!"

Not Mice!

We do not like mice. We do not like mice!

In a yard, mice will eat plants and nuts. Mice like a nice seed meal.

In a home, mice will eat what we like. They eat cheese, meat, rice, cider, corn, and sweets.

But mice seem to eat stuff we will not eat.

They seem to like bits of wire, lace, or a box. But mice only bite these to get to a place or treat.

Mice are not big or long. They can fit into a thin space in a fence. They can fit in a hole the size of a cent!

Since we do not like mice, we trap them. We get rid of them. We are not nice to mice.

A Big Barn Fire!

A din in the goose pen woke me up. I stuck on boots and ran to the yard. The barn was on fire! That goose pen was not at that barn. It was safe.

That fire was not big yet, but it would be soon. I called 911 on my cell and then ran in that hot barn.

I led a horse to the yard. Fire shot through the barn roof. Thick smoke hid the moon. I would have been a fool to zoom back in that barn.

Fire trucks came, but too late. That big red barn fell.

At noon, I stand at that barn mess. I know what it takes to make a new barn. I will do it.

A Loon

Do you know what a loon is? It is a bird like a duck or goose.

A loon can seem odd when it is on land. It acts a bit like a fool. Can it be called a loon for that?

But in a lake, a loon is smooth and cool. As it hunts for food, it can make long dives through deep, deep lakes. It will hunt for a fish or bug meal. It will grab a frog too.

A loon has cool black and white checks or stripes on its back. It can have a red neck and black beak.

Need proof that a loon is not a fool? See if you can spot one in a zoo!

A Bike Ride

Chad had a map. "Mike, we can do this! It is called a coast-to-coast bike ride. We can make this a goal!" he said.

"You mean we would ride bikes on a road west to east? That is a load of miles!" said Mike.

"Yes, we would take packs. We would load them with coats, shirts, snacks, and soap!" said Chad.

"We would roast if we rode through hot spots," said Mike.

"I know, but we would stop to loaf and float in cool lakes. And when we get back home, we can boast!" said Mike.

In a bit, Mike said, "Chad, I do not have a bike."

Chad said, "Do not feel bad. I cannot ride one!"

Do Goats Eat Tin?

Is it a fact that a goat will eat a tin can? A goat will not. But goats will taste lots of odd stuff.

Goats will lick soap, your coat, foam on a pipe, or a loaf of bread. If they like the taste, they will munch a bit. Goats do not know that a taste of foam or soap can make them sick.

On a farm, goats roam and eat what they see, such as bark or a leaf. They will sniff through plants. Goats will eat green grass.

Goats need to eat corn, oats, or wheat. On a farm, they will be fed these. They will not be fed a tin can!

Quack

"Quack! Quack!"

It was those ducks! Quinn stuck the quilt on his head. Through the quilt, he called, "Quit it, you ducks!"

"Quack! Quack!" Those ducks did not quit.

Quinn did like this trip to the lake with Dad. He did like ducks. But Quinn did not like quacks just as the sun came up!

The trip was quite a lot of fun. Quinn got to fish and joke with Dad. Quinn was sad when it had to end.

At home, Quinn had no ducks, just class and a big quiz. A quiz! Quinn had to get up but did not.

"Quack! Quack!"

That made Quinn jump up. Then he got it.

"I know that was you, Dad!" said Quinn.

"Quack," said Dad.

Quilt Art

Do you have a quilt on a bed at home? A quilt can be quite nice. A quilt can be called art.

A quilt can have just one big shape on it, such as a star or moon.

Or a quilt can have square blocks. Each square can be the same. Each can have the same duck and term "Quack" on it.

But the blocks do not have to be the same. One square can have a fast car. One can have a quick van. That quilt can have trucks, ships, jets, and more.

It can be hard to make a quilt. A quilt for a queen-size bed takes a lot of time. Do not quit! Make quilt art!

Fred's

Dad fills lunch bags. He asks, "Why do we not have bread and cheese?"

Dad sends me to Fred's Food Store. As I leave, Dad yells, "Fred's will close at five!"

When I get to Fred's, he sees me. Then I see Miss Rose. She has bags. I set them in her car.

As I rush in Fred's, Gramps Stone drops six cans. Fred sees me pick those up. But the store clock ticks.

Then I see that little James cannot reach the peas. I get them. Fred's clock chimes five. Yikes!

I have no cheese or bread, but Fred's will close! I must leave.

Fred stops me. "We do not close at five for nice kids. Take your time."

I am glad!

Dart Frogs

Dart frogs are cute. These frogs are little, just an inch or so in size. Their skins shine in nice blends of reds, greens, blacks, tans, and more. That means it is hard for these frogs to hide.

But do not let these cute frogs fool you. Please do not kiss one! This is why. A dart frog's skin kills. If a snake licks a dart frog's skin, that snake is dead. So when snakes, bats, or birds see dart frogs in trees, they know it is wise to leave.

A dart frog's skin can kill us, too. Yet do not fret. These frogs are not close to us.

But it is still wise not to kiss a frog!

You can tell that the train made its turn way too fast. That is why these five box cars are on their sides and not on the rails. Speed made them tip.

I am glad to say that no one was hurt. But these cars will block the tracks. It may take a little time to get them back up on the rails. That will make more trains late. Those trains need to stay back and wait.

We do have a way to set these cars back on the rails. That is my job. I run a big crane that rides on the rails.

With chains, my crane will lift these cars and set them on the tracks. It will take a day.

Slime

What stays in a shell and makes slime trails? A snail!

A snail's shell is not thick at first. But as the snail gains in size, its shell gets hard as a rock.

A snail has a little brain. Is a snail smart? Can you train it to do tricks? Pet shops claim you can a bit.

Snail slime is cool! A snail oozes a slime trail and slides on it. Slime aids a snail in more ways. With slime, a snail can stay on a cliff or a fence side.

Slime can save a snail's life. A snail makes more slime when a bird or frog plans to eat it. The snail sprays slime foam. Why? Slime foam tastes bad! Yuck!

Dreams

At night, my sis Jean and I lie on grass. We gaze up. Bright stars fill the night sky. I say, "This is a good night!"

"It is nice!" Jean tells me.

"When I see these stars, I dream of jets," I say. "If I can fly high in the sky, I will see bright stars flash by. I might try to fly jets."

"That would be good work," Jean tells me.

"When you see the sky, Jean, do you have any dreams?" I ask.

Jean sighs. "Pie! I dream of pie!"

I sit up. I say, "Pie! Why pie?"

"I like Mom's good peach pie!" Jean tells me.

"Yes!" I say. "Let's go ask Mom for more pie!"

And we do.

A Drone

The drone is in flight. It is high in the sky.

A drone is like a little plane. It might seem like a big bug to you. Mice might just fit in it.

The man who flies the drone stands on land. Through the drone cam, he sees what his drone sees. The drone is a spy.

The man flies the drone by a dam. The dam keeps a deep lake safe. If the dam has any leaks, a team must work to fix them.

With a cam on his drone, the man can check the dam. It seems like he is right at the side of the dam.

The man cannot see any leaks. The dam is dry. That is good!

Fair!

The paper had an ad for the fair at Ames Square. April and I had to go!

I like fair games. At the first game, I did not win. April did. Her prize was a cat with green hair.

At game two, I did not win. April did. This prize was a pair of fake bugs.

I did not play more games. April did. Her prizes were good chains, aprons for her dad's work, and hair clips. April did not share any.

Then we went on a ride. It spun us on chairs high in the air. It did not scare April. It did me. April had fun. I got sick. I had to leave!

My day at the fair was not fair.

Jets!

At Air Fest, fans sit on sand, papers, and beach chairs. They share stone stairs. They sit on tables!

In the air, those who fly jets are brave. They fly with flair. They dare big risks.

Six jets fly in the shape of a square. They shine in the sun's glare.

Then the jets speed in pairs. One pair seems too close! Did the two jets hit? One flies up, but one dives! Black smoke trails it. Will it crash? Will it be able to go up? Fans stare. This dive scares them!

Then the jet turns up to the sky. Good! It sprays red and green smoke flares. Five jets meet it. Six jets whiz close to the beach. Fans clap and yell.

Stairs

We had to pack. But first we made space in the van.

Dad had spare tires. One had no air. Dad set it by his bench. I had hair care stuff on the back seat. "Please set it by the bath, Clare," Mom said.

I ran up the stairs.

Mom and Dad did fast work. They set a big box on the stairs. They set a kid's chair by it. They set square frames and pairs of skates on a step. They set more on the stairs.

"Clare, the van is bare," said Mom. "We can pack. Run back."

I was at the top of the stairs. Stuff was on each step! "I cannot, Mom. I cannot see any stairs," I said.

We sit on chairs in the night air. We stare at a pair of dim lights high in the sky. They each flare up! Each is bright! Then each fades in the dark.

They did not scare us. But what were they?

They were space craft. They fly high in the sky and do good work for us. They aid us as we speak on cells.

When these craft are on land, their sides shine in the sun. That glare is bright.

As these craft fly high in the sky, light of the sun can hit them. At night, we do not see the sun. But we do see its light on these craft. We see the flare that the light makes.

A Gray Ship

Gene and Mom stand on the huge bridge. It is so high! When ships go past, Gene sees in them. One large ship has huge trucks on it. He sees men and things on the ship.

Gene leans on the edge of the bridge rail. He spots a gray ship. It is not close yet. It is just a gray speck. Should Gene tap Mom? Is this the ship?

Gene will not budge. He has to see this ship. Soon it is at close range. Its flag is high in the sky. Its horn blares.

Is this the ship?

Gene was just age nine when Dad left. Gene was so sad.

The ship is close. Gene can see men on it waving. He can see Dad! Dad has come back! Gene and Mom wave. Dad is safe!

Hard Work

Long Beach Port is a seaport. Huge ships sail there. As ships come in, they line up on the edge of long docks.

Each ship has large loads of things. Those loads must go on trains and trucks. Roads and train tracks are right on the dock.

And on the dock sits a large frame. It seems like a mix of a bridge and a cage. Big cranes slide on this frame. They can slide to the top of a ship.

The crane picks up a big box on the ship. It then sets the box on a rail car or truck.

The man who runs the crane must be able to judge where to set each box. He should not nudge any trains or trucks. He hopes not to drop a large box of cars, TVs, or fudge. It is hard work.

At Sea

Max and Gus did not feel safe at sea.
Their little boat did not have much fuel.
The air felt humid. The sky was dark.
A storm would come.

"We should get back fast," said Gus.

But Gus and Max may have been too late.
As they sped to shore, huge waves drove
the boat back.

Then things got very bad. Max had used
a lot of fuel to fight those waves. Now no
fuel was left. Wind made the boat spin.
Rain fell hard. Would these men make it
back? They did not know.

Then a horn blast cut through the storm.
Was it music?

"Unit One! This is Unit Six!"

Who said that?

"We see a boat with two men. We will take them and their boat to shore."

A big boat came through rain and waves. Finally, Gus and Max were safe.

Play Music!

Are you a music pupil? If not, take a class that will teach you to play. Or find a music tutor. You might play a bugle or a French horn. You might play a flute or a sax. You can be a drummer.

If you play well, you might get in a band. A band unites you with more music students. You might be in a class band that plays on a stage. You can be in a band that plays at team games. You might be in a band that plays on TV and CDs.

Not each kid can play music well. If you cannot, you can still be a music pupil. A music class will teach you how music works. It will teach you kinds of music.

We know that music can help the human brain. It makes you smart. You should be a music pupil!

Mitch

Mitch feels like a Hide-and-Seek pro. If he is "it," he spots the rest of the kids fast. If he is not "it," no one can catch him.

Mitch brags to his Mom. "When I was 'it,' I did not chase the kids. I just said where each one was."

Mom sees red spots on Mitch's hands. Do those spots itch?

"Another time, I hid in a ditch. I had to stretch to stay flat in it. The kids just ran around me. Then they ran away," Mitch adds.

Mitch has red spots on his arms, too. They match those on his hands. Mom tells him, "That ditch has plants that scratch and might make a rash. Do your hands and arms itch?"

"Yes, Mom."

Mom rubs cream on Mitch's hands and arms.

"I am still the best, Mom," he adds.

A Hen Egg

When will a chick hatch?

An eggshell has an air cell in it. In the egg, the chick will need that air. Its head must switch to face the cell. When the chick gets big, it pops the cell with its beak. The chick will then catch its first air. But it needs more.

With its beak, the chick will scratch and hit the shell. It will hit it a lot. With long work, the chick will make a hole in the shell. The chick will rest.

But the chick still needs more air. So its itch to be free grows. The chick turns around in the eggshell. As it turns, it chips hard at the eggshell. As it chips, it will stretch and stretch to get that shell away. When that shell has big cracks, it will be hatch time. Another chick is free!

Gramps

Gramps was by his trees. He grew plants. He had quite a few trees around his yard, too. "Hi, Gramps!" I said.

"Hi, Tom," said Gramps, as he gave me a hug.

"Are a few of these trees new?" I said.

"Yes, Tom," Gramps said. "I just had a tree crew plant them."

"What is this little tree?" I said.

"It is a yew tree," said Gramps.

"A you tree!" I said. "Do you mean me? A Tom tree?"

That made Gramps grin. "No, not that kind of you. It is a yew. You spell it Y-E-W," he said.

"Cool!" I said.

Then I spot another tree. It had white blooms. "What is that?" I said.

Gramps had a grin. He ran his hand through his white hair and said, "It is a Gramps tree. It is white on top and not new!"

My Gramps makes the best jokes!

Fire!

Smoke blew high in the sky. At first, just a few trees were on fire. But the fire grew.

A fire plane flew around the huge park to check what the flames might burn.

A wide road was on one side of the fire. Flames should not jump past that. Still, a fire crew was sent to the road. They had pumps and hoses.

On another side was a patch of little yews. Those yews might be more fuel for the fire. A large part of the crew was sent with tools. They had to get rid of those yews!

Just west of the fire was a big ditch. It had dead, dry trees in it. The fire might use them as fuel too. A crew had to burn them away. If they did not, this fire would spread.

The crews act fast. This fire will not last long.

Paws?

In late March, a thaw set in. The chill was not bad.
Lawns were not green yet. That would take time.

The bike trail was mud, ice, bits of straw, and
dead leaves. Most kids would not ride a bike yet,
but I did. As I rode, raw wind froze my face.

I went around a turn on the trail and saw a dog
run away. Or was it a dog? I saw fresh paw prints.
Those paws had claws. What had made them?

I had my cam with me. I had to crawl a bit in the
mud to get a shot of the prints.

At home, Dad and I went on the Web to find
those paw prints. Those were not dog paws.
A bobcat made them!

Dad said that bobcats hide. They hope humans
do not see them. Good! I hope they stay away.

Bobcats

Do bobcats hide around your home? A bobcat is twice as big as a pet cat. But you may not see a bobcat. It is a hunter. It hides well.

A bobcat is not too long, but its legs are. Its back legs are bent and thick so it can jump and run fast. Its paws and claws are big, too.

But when it hunts, a bobcat stays down and seems to crawl. Then it leaps. The bad news is that if a bobcat saw a pup on your lawn, it might leap and get it! A bobcat will eat birds, mice, and more. With its teeth and jaws, it can eat fawns and snakes too.

Bobcats hunt at night and rest at dawn. Most bobcats will not bite humans. But a sick bobcat might. Do not get close to a bobcat!

Snow

Jill and Flo were at Flo's home. In the yard, snow fell.

"I will show you snow globes I own," said Flo.

Flo was known for snow globes. "A globe is a bit like a glass bowl," said Flo.

"I know," said Jill.

In Flo's yard, snow still fell.

"This one shows kids on skates. You shake the globe and snow floats. I found this at a yard sale," said Flo.

"This one shows New York. It glows. You shake this globe and snow floats," said Flo.

Real snow still fell in the yard.

"This one shows a bird, a crow. You shake this globe," said Flo.

"I know! And snow floats!" said Jill.

In the yard, snow still fell. As Flo got another globe off a shelf, Jill said, "Let's go play in real snow!"

"Real snow! No!" said Flo. "I like snow in globes, not on me!"

Fish That Glow

A few fish glow. They are found in deep parts of the sea. Not much light is that low. A glow might be seen in those dark seas.

We know that fish eat fish. So why would a fish glow and show off?

A fish might glow to trick another fish. A glow might make another fish swim close. Then crunch! That fish is lunch.

Or fish glow to make another fish go away. One sort of shrimp is known to throw up bits of stuff that glows. That chases away a fish that might eat it.

Fish glow to hide, too. In the dark part of the sea, you see dim sunlight. The glow of a little fish might match the light. So when big fish swim low,

they will not see that little one. They just flow
past it.

Toy Drive

Roy set a box in the Toy Team truck. It was the last toy for the toy drive.

Gray Hills was known for this toy drive. Moms, dads, boys, and girls of Gray Hills gave toys. The toys go to kids who do not have much. These toys would fill kids' lives with joy.

That night, Gray Hills TV had bad news. A man drove off with the Toy Team truck! On TV, Roy said, "We hope he hands those toys to kids who need them."

The bad news made Gray Hills' moms, dads, boys, and girls act fast. In a week, they gave the Toy Team three more truckloads of toys.

At the end of that week, Roy found the first Toy Team truck. Its load of toys was back, too! On TV, Roy said, "I know that loads of toys will mean loads of joy!"

Soy

As you drive past farms, you see soybean plants. They are green and grow in rows. They may grow six feet high.

Soy is a big part of your life! As you drive away, you might not know that.

Soy is in foods you eat. In one way or another, you eat soy most days. It might be in ice cream, bread, or rolls.

On farms, pigs, goats, sheep, and chicks eat soy feed. On fish farms, fish do. Soy is in pet food, too. Soy is in fuel for cars, trucks, trains, and planes. It might keep the price of fuel low. Soy can be in paint and soap.

Do you know those plush toys that little boys and girls hug with joy?

They might be made with soy. So might toy cars and planes.

Check around. Can you find more ways we use soy?

The Best Sauce

"This is my sauce plan," said Deke.

"A sauce plan?" said Joan. "What is a sauce plan?"

"It is my plan to make the best sauce! It will be a sauce that is a top seller!" said Deke.

"How will this plan work?" said Joan.

"First, I will make the sauce. It will be known as the best sauce!" said Deke.

"But what . . . ?" said Joan.

"Then trucks will haul my sauce to stores. Stores will sell it. I will make so much cash!" said Deke.

"But what . . . ?" said Joan.

"I will keep a bit of that cash. The rest I will hand off to good causes that aid kids!" said Deke.

"But what is in this sauce?" said Joan.

"That is the one fault in my plan," said Deke. "I do not know a way to make the best sauce!"

Quakes

Have you felt a quake shake your street or home? What causes quakes?

For a long time, we have known the cause. Waves that pass through rocks cause quakes. These waves are a bit like sea waves, but in the land.

But what causes those waves?

The top part of the globe is its crust. The crust is made of large rock blocks or plates. The globe has lots of rock plates. Spots where these plates meet are known as faults.

At times, these rock plates slide a bit. They slide and pause, slide and pause. That will not cause a quake. But as the plates slide, one plate might ram another plate at a fault. Bam! That crash might cause waves in the land. Those waves make the quake that shakes streets and homes.

Tess

The music hall has rows and rows of seats. A few moms and dads sit in them, but they do not fill them all.

It is a nice fall day. In the park by the hall, it is a day to play baseball or take long walks. It is not a day to sit in a music hall.

But on the music hall stage, Tess is glad to play. She makes sweet music with her flute. When her notes float to the seats, moms and dads smile. When her notes float to the park, kids put baseballs and bats away. Games stop, and long walks end.

More moms, dads, boys, and girls walk into the hall. They all had thought this was a nice day for the park. But as Tess plays, they all sit. They take every seat. It is a nice day for sweet music, too.

Green Walls

Have you seen walls made of live green plants?
These walls can be in halls, homes, and malls.
These walls can be wide or tall. Each seems like a
backyard patch of green plants put up on its side!

Why do we have live walls like these?

As green plants grow on these walls, they do a lot.
On hot days, these plants fight the heat. They keep
a room cool.

On freezing days, green plants on the wall fight the
chill. They keep a room nice and cozy.

Every day, live plant walls will clean the air in
classrooms, halls, or malls. Clean air is good for each
of us!

With live walls, we use less fuel to cool or heat a
room. If we use less fuel, we save cash and the
globe.

One last thought: We do not need to paint live walls.
We just trim them!

Chimes

At every hour, the round clock on Smith Hall would chime. At five, it would chime five times. At ten, it would chime ten.

Paul's house was by Smith Hall. Paul did not like hour chimes. Loud chimes would tell him to get up. They would tell him when to bake bread. Chimes sent Paul to bed at night. Chimes ran Paul the baker's life!

One night, dark clouds came. Rain fell. A loud flash hit the clock. It crashed to the ground!

At first, Paul thought this was good. Chimes did not count each hour. Loud sounds did not wake Paul, tell him to bake, or make him go to bed. Soon Paul got up late each day, did not bake bread, and did not sleep. He was a mess.

One day, Smith Hall had new sounds. Pound! Pound! Paul was pounding. He had to put that clock back up!

Just a Little Rain?

We count on rain. But at times, rain will not fall. Then days get and stay hot. The ground dries. Plants, crops, and grass die. Lakes and ponds grow small. Fish like trout and bass may die.

With no rain, we do not bathe much or use hoses to fill our pools. We gaze out at the sky for clouds. But the sun just shines for long hours. Every cloud just floats by. We still do not get rain. Not a drop is found.

If rain still will not fall, we might send airplanes up to any clouds we see. The airplanes can put ice or a kind of seed in those clouds. Ice or those seeds might chill the clouds. If the clouds do get cold, raindrops may form. Those raindrops may fall to the ground.

The sound of rain would make us glad.

Cold?

A chill wind blows in the ball park.
Rich feels like he might freeze.

"Ump, can I ask a dumb thing? Is it
too cold to play baseball?" asks Rich.

"Too cold? That is dumb!" the umpire
yells. "The sun is out. The heat will
climb!"

Rich's hands freeze.

"Play ball!" yells the umpire.

The first Cub at bat hits the ball hard!
Rich grabs it in the air. The umpire
puts up his thumb and yells, "Out!"

Snow falls a bit. "It is not time for
snowflakes. It is still fall!" the umpire
yells.

The next Cub hits the ball to Rich, too.
Rich throws him out. The umpire puts his
thumb up and yells, "Out!"

Now the umpire is cold. He puts his
thumb up. It is numb. He tells Rich, "I will
tell you a not-so-dumb thing. It is too cold!
We will stop this game!"

Thumbs

We use the term *thumb* in odd ways.

If I say you have a *green thumb*, should you clean it? No. If you have a green thumb, it means your vines climb high and roses smell sweet. It means every seed you plant in the backyard grows well.

If I am *all thumbs,* it means that I may not do things well. So I might tell you, "When I try to comb my dog's hair, I am all thumbs!"

If you climb up a tree to save a cat, I might show you a *thumbs up*. That means I thought you did a nice thing.

If you drop popcorn crumbs on my new rug, I will show you a *thumbs down*. You know what that means!

If I tell you to sweep up those crumbs, you might *thumb your nose* at me. That means you did not like what I said.

What Kate Knows

"Did you know that dogs have knees on their back legs?" Jess asks Kate.

"Yes, I know that. That is why dogs can sit," Kate tells Jess.

"Did you know why a square knot is not a safe knot?" Jess asks Kate.

"Yes, I know that. Although it may not seem like it, that knot can slip," Kate tells Jess.

"Did you know that the term *knit* came from an old term for *knot*?" Jess asks Kate.

"Yes, I know that. And in old times, only men would knit," Kate tells Jess.

"Do you know what my house cats once had a knack for?" Jess asks Kate.

"Yes, I know that. They felt it was fun to knock houseplants on the rug," Kate tells Jess.

"You know too much stuff! Do you know that I do not like that?" Jess asks Kate.

"Yes, I know that," Kate tells Jess again.

Storm!

A big storm can be bad. It can knock houses to bits.

You know that in a storm, you must find a safe place in your house. Stay in the basement. Or kneel low on your knees in a bathtub or below a desktop.

If you are on a highway in a car, get out! Lie flat in a ditch on the ground.

Stay safe while the storm rages. Once the storm ends, you still must stay safe.

When a storm ends, your backyard may be a mess. You may see bits of bricks or steel that are as sharp as knives. It is possible you will see wires that spark. Stay away! Although the storm has blown past, you can still get hurt.

Outside you may see things that once were far away. Your knickknacks may be blocks away! You might get them again. Safety first!

Look!

Josh and Mom sat by a brook in the woods. A nice breeze shook the leaves.

On a hill by the brook, a man and his kids stood still. Josh saw them. But they did not look at him or Mom. Josh did not know what they saw. Then a small bird flew up in the sky. Josh and Mom saw it as it took off.

"Did you get a good look?" said the man to his kids. "You might not see it again. This might be a once in a lifetime treat!"

Then the man and kids came down to the brook. The kids had bird books. "What did you see?" Mom said.

"A wood thrush!" said a girl. "It is a rare, rare bird!"

Although Josh did not know bird facts, Mom did.
She said to the girl, "That is so cool!"

So were walks with Mom.

Sod Homes

In the Old West, it was hard to make a house. Good wood was hard to find. So houses were made of sod.

If you cut a square foot of grass out of a lawn, it will be both grass and dirt. That is sod, although it will not look like Old West sod.

In the Old West, sod was thick and hard to cut out of the land. The grass had deep, thick roots. It took plows and horses to cut out sod. Sod might have hoofprints on it!

Men would stack thick sod bricks to make walls. Sod made good walls but not good roofs. Once the roof was up, men would fix it again and again.

A sod house might have three rooms. It was safe to cook in. And once it was up, it was not too cold or hot. It was home, sweet home!

Go to Seed?

Do you know the phrase "let it go to seed"? It means not to take care of things.

If you do not take care of a doghouse, you "let it go to seed."

If a phone has dents and nicks, you "let it go to seed."

Why do we say that? Will a doghouse or phone turn into seeds? No, but a plant will.

A plant's life has phases. In phase one, it is a seed. In phase two, the seed starts to grow.

In phase three, the plant grows up. In the last phase, it blooms.

Once its blooms die, the plant makes new seeds. So it will again go to seed.

If you do not take care of plants, they go to seed too fast. They look bad. If you do not take care of a doghouse or phone, they look bad, too.

Phones

Do you have a phone? In times past, most kids did not. Most grown-ups did not!

Phones were first made in the 1870s. They used wires known as phone lines. Sound would pass through these lines. Back then, you might use phrases like "I am on the line."

Phones were not everywhere. Poles and wires had to be set up. That set-up phase took much time.

Even then, calls were not made to far-off places. But once phone cables were set in deep seas, calls were made around the globe.

In the 1980s, a few phones did not need wires. These cordless phones

were like cell phones, although they would work only inside homes. Homes still had phone lines.

Now we use cell phones. We do not need lines. Our sounds are in waves that we cannot see. But do not use the phrase "I am on the wave!"

Wilbur and Orville

The bike shop had been good for Wilbur and Orville Wright. They did not just fix bikes. They made them. But as Orville turned a wrench, he would dream of airplanes. As Wilbur wrote plans for bikes, he would write plans for flight, too.

It was 1896, and airplanes did not fly yet. The Wrights hoped they might make one.

Did they know enough? The bike shop had taught them things that would help. They read a lot, too. They knew how gliders might fly.

Then sad news came. A man died in a glider wreck. He had hopes to fly, too.

News of the wreck did not end the Wrights' dream. It made them work harder and read more. They wrote to men who had the same dream. They asked what works with gliders. What does not? Why? The Wrights made plans. Would they fly?

Would this be the day? Would humans write that this was the day that a real airplane flew?

Orville and Wilbur Wright were on the seashore. A small airplane sat on wood tracks. Well, it was an airplane if it would fly. Wilbur had tried to fly the airplane. That flight failed, but it taught the Wrights a few things.

Now it was Orville's turn. What did he feel? "Did we do enough? Will this fly? If it does, will I die in a wreck?"

Wilbur and a few men got the airplane set. Its motor began to run. Ropes still kept it on the ground.

The ropes fell off. The motor made the airplane go up. Orville flew! The airplane did bob up and down a bit, but it flew. On December 17, 1903, a human flew for the first time.

Write it down. This was the day!

Sound/Spelling(s) and High-Frequency Words by Selection

Selection 1: Sam

Sound/Spelling(s) Introduced: /a/ spelled *a*, /m/ spelled *m*, /s/ spelled *s*, /t/ spelled *t, tt*

Selection 2: Matt

Sound/Spelling(s) Reviewed: /a/ spelled *a*, /m/ spelled *m*, /s/ spelled *s*, /t/ spelled *t, tt*

Selection 3: Sass?

Sound/Spelling(s) Introduced: /d/ spelled *d*, /s/ spelled *ss*

Selection 4: Dad at Dam

Sound/Spelling(s) Reviewed: /d/ spelled *d*, /a/ spelled *a*, /m/ spelled *m*, /s/ spelled *s*, /t/ spelled *t*

Selection 5: Sad Tam, Mad Ed

Sound/Spelling(s) Introduced: /ĕ/ spelled *e*

High-Frequency Words Introduced: he, she

Selection 6: Mess?

Sound/Spelling(s) Reviewed: /ĕ/ spelled *e*, /d/ spelled *d*, /a/ spelled *a*, /m/ spelled *m*, /s/ spelled *s, ss;* /t/ spelled *t*

High-Frequency Words Reviewed: he

Selection 7: Fast Tad

Sound/Spelling(s) Introduced: /f/ spelled *f, ff*

High-Frequency Words Introduced: a

Selection 8: Tess Fed Stems

Sound/Spelling(s) Reviewed: /f/ spelled *f*, /ĕ/ spelled *e*, /d/ spelled *d*, /a/ spelled *a*, /m/ spelled *m*, /s/ spelled *s, ss;* /t/ spelled *t*

High-Frequency Words Reviewed: she

Selection 9: Stef's Cam

Sound/Spelling(s) Introduced: /k/ spelled *c*

Selection 10: Cat Facts

Sound/Spelling(s) Reviewed: /k/ spelled *c*, /f/ spelled *f*, /ĕ/ spelled *e*, /d/ spelled *d*, /a/ spelled *a*, /m/ spelled *m*, /s/ spelled *s*, /t/ spelled *t*

High-Frequency Words Reviewed: she

Selection 11: The Mitt

Sound/Spelling(s) Introduced: /ĭ/ spelled *i*

High-Frequency Words Introduced: the, is

Selection 12: Miss Stam's Act

Sound/Spelling(s) Reviewed: /ĭ/ spelled *i*, /k/ spelled *c*, /ĕ/ spelled *e*, /d/ spelled *d*, /a/ spelled *a*, /m/ spelled *m*, /s/ spelled *s*, *ss*; /t/ spelled *t*

High-Frequency Words Reviewed: the, he, is

Selection 13: Red Raft

Sound/Spelling(s) Introduced: /r/ spelled *r*

High-Frequency Words Reviewed: the

Selection 14: Dim Mist

Sound/Spelling(s) Reviewed: /r/ spelled *r*, /ĭ/ spelled *i*, /f/ spelled *f*, /ĕ/ spelled *e*, /d/ spelled *d*, *dd*; /a/ spelled *a*, /m/ spelled *m*, /s/ spelled *s*, /t/ spelled *t*

High-Frequency Words Introduced: we

Selection 15: A Hat? A Dress?

Sound/Spelling(s) Introduced: /h/ spelled *h*

High-Frequency Words Reviewed: he, she, the

Selection 16: Hiss!

Sound/Spelling(s) Reviewed: /h/ spelled *h*, /r/ spelled *r*, /ĭ/ spelled *i*, /k/ spelled *c*, /f/ spelled *f*, /ĕ/ spelled *e*, /d/ spelled *d*, /a/ spelled *a*, /m/ spelled *m*, /s/ spelled *s*, *ss*; /t/ spelled *t*

High-Frequency Words Introduced: has

Selection 17: Cams and Rafts

Sound/Spelling(s) Introduced: /th/ (voiced) spelled *th*

High-Frequency Words Introduced: and

Selection 18: *Mist*

Sound/Spelling(s) Reviewed: /th/ (voiced) spelled *th*, /h/ spelled *h*, /r/ spelled *r*, /ĭ/ spelled *i*, /k/ spelled *c*, /f/ spelled *f*, /ĕ/ spelled *e*, /d/ spelled *d*, /a/ spelled *a*, /m/ spelled *m*, /s/ spelled *s*, *ss*; /t/ spelled *t*, *tt*

High-Frequency Words Introduced: to

Selection 19: Red Dots!

Sound/Spelling(s) Introduced: /ŏ/ spelled *o*

High-Frequency Words Introduced: of

Selection 20: Odd Todd

Sound/Spelling(s) Reviewed: /ŏ/ spelled *o*, /th/ (voiced) spelled *th*, /h/ spelled *h*, /r/ spelled *r*, /ĭ/ spelled *i*, /f/ spelled *f*, /ĕ/ spelled *e*, /d/ spelled *d*, *dd*; /a/ spelled *a*, /m/ spelled *m*, /s/ spelled *s*, *ss*; /t/ spelled *t*

High-Frequency Words Reviewed: and, he, she, the

Selection 21: Can Nan?

Sound/Spelling(s) Introduced: /n/ spelled *n*

High-Frequency Words Reviewed: to, and

Selection 22: Ants and Ham

Sound/Spelling(s) Reviewed: /n/ spelled *n*, /ŏ/ spelled *o*, /th/ (voiced) spelled *th*, /h/ spelled *h*, /r/ spelled *r*, /ĭ/ spelled *i*, /k/ spelled *c*, /f/ spelled *f*, /ĕ/ spelled *e*, /d/ spelled *d*, /a/ spelled *a*, /m/ spelled *m*, /s/ spelled *s*, /t/ spelled *t*

High-Frequency Words Reviewed: to, and, the, of

Selection 23: Sit!

Sound/Spelling(s) Introduced: /b/ spelled *b*

High-Frequency Words Introduced: you

Selection 24: Fast!

Sound/Spelling(s) Reviewed: /b/ spelled *b*, /n/ spelled *n*, /th/ (voiced) spelled *th*, /h/ spelled *h*, /r/ spelled *r*, /ĭ/ spelled *i*, /k/ spelled *c*, /f/ spelled *f*, /ĕ/ spelled *e*, /d/ spelled *d*, /a/ spelled *a*, /m/ spelled *m*, /s/ spelled *s*, /t/ spelled *t*

High-Frequency Words Reviewed: is, the, a, and

Selection 25: Socks?

Sound/Spelling(s) Introduced: /k/ spelled *ck*

High-Frequency Words Reviewed: is, a, you, the

Selection 26: Rocks Hit Fast!

Sound/Spelling(s) Reviewed: /k/ spelled *ck, c*; /b/ spelled *b*, /n/ spelled *n*, /ŏ/ spelled *o*, /th/ (voiced) spelled *th*, /h/ spelled *h*, /r/ spelled *r*, /ĭ/ spelled *i*, /f/ spelled *f*, /ĕ/ spelled *e*, /d/ spelled *d*, /a/ spelled *a*, /m/ spelled *m*, /s/ spelled *s*, *ss*; /t/ spelled *t*

High-Frequency Words Reviewed: is, we, the, of, a

Selection 27: A Wet West Wind

Sound/Spelling(s) Introduced: /w/ spelled *w_*

High-Frequency Words Reviewed: she, of, the, a, and

Selection 28: Mick and Mack on the Web

Sound/Spelling(s) Reviewed: /w/ spelled *w_*, /k/ spelled *ck*, /b/ spelled *b*, /n/ spelled *n*, /ŏ/ spelled *o*, /h/ spelled *h*, /r/ spelled *r*, /ĭ/ spelled *i*, /f/ spelled *f*, /ĕ/ spelled *e*, /d/ spelled *d*, /a/ spelled *a*, /m/ spelled *m*, /s/ spelled *s*, *ss*; /t/ spelled *t*

High-Frequency Words Introduced: as

Selection 29: A Dish Stack

Sound/Spelling(s) Introduced: /sh/ spelled *sh*

High-Frequency Words Introduced: I, was

Selection 30: A Shock!

Sound/Spelling(s) Reviewed: /sh/ spelled *sh*, /w/ spelled *w_*, /k/ spelled *c, ck;* /b/ spelled *b*, /n/ spelled *n*, /ŏ/ spelled *o*, /th/ (voiced) spelled *th*, /r/ spelled *r*, /ĭ/ spelled *i*, /f/ spelled *f*, /ĕ/ spelled *e*, /d/ spelled *d*, /a/ spelled *a*, /m/ spelled *m*, /s/ spelled *s*, *ss;* /t/ spelled *t*

High-Frequency Words Introduced: be

Selection 31: Not Me!

Sound/Spelling(s) Introduced: /ē/ spelled *e*

High-Frequency Words Introduced: me, said

Selection 32: Mack and Beck!

Sound/Spelling(s) Introduced: /th/ (unvoiced) spelled *th*

High-Frequency Words Reviewed: said, the, is, he, she, be, a, and

Selection 33: A "G" Hat

Sound/Spelling(s) Introduced: /g/ spelled *g*

High-Frequency Words Reviewed: the, was, I, a, and, to, he, you, is, be

Selection 34: Grant and the Frog

Sound/Spelling(s) Reviewed: /g/ spelled *g*, ē spelled *e*, /k/ spelled *ck, c;* /b/ spelled *b*, /n/ spelled *n*, /ŏ/ spelled *o*, /th/ (voiced) spelled *th*, /h/ spelled *h*, /r/ spelled *r*, /ĭ/ spelled *i*, /f/ spelled *f*, /ĕ/ spelled *e*, /d/ spelled *dd*, /a/ spelled *a*, /s/ spelled *s*, /t/ spelled *t*

High-Frequency Words Reviewed: was, the, to, is, a, he, and

Selection 35: Snacks in a Bag

Sound/Spelling(s) Introduced: /ō/ spelled *o*

High-Frequency Words Introduced: are

Selection 36: Fast?

Sound/Spelling(s) Reviewed: /ō/ spelled *o*, /g/ spelled *g*, /sh/ spelled *sh*, /w/ spelled *w_*, /k/ spelled *ck, c;* /f/ spelled *f*, /b/ spelled *b*, /n/ spelled *n*, /ŏ/ spelled *o*, /th/ (voiced) spelled *th*, /r/ spelled *r*, /ĭ/ spelled *i*, /ĕ/ spelled *e*, /d/ spelled *d*, /a/ spelled *a*, /s/ spelled *s*, /t/ spelled *t*

High-Frequency Words Introduced: or

Selection 37: Damp Camp

Sound/Spelling(s) Introduced: /p/ spelled *p*

High-Frequency Words Reviewed: the, was, or, is, said, I, to, a, she, we, and

Selection 38: A Pest Pig

Sound/Spelling(s) Reviewed: /p/ spelled p, /sh/ spelled sh, /g/ spelled g, /ē/ spelled e, /k/ spelled ck, c; /f/ spelled f, /b/ spelled b, /n/ spelled n, /ŏ/ spelled o, /th/ (voiced) spelled th, /r/ spelled r, /ĭ/ spelled i, /f/ spelled f, /ĕ/ spelled e, /d/ spelled d, /a/ spelled a, /m/ spelled m, /s/ spelled s, ss; /t/ spelled t

High-Frequency Words Reviewed: the, or, is, a, and, be

Selection 39: Fern

Sound/Spelling(s) Introduced: /er/ spelled er

High-Frequency Words Reviewed: was, the, to, a, she, and, as

Selection 40: A Ship

Sound/Spelling(s) Reviewed: /er/ spelled er, /g/ spelled g, /w/ spelled w_, /k/ spelled ck, /f/ spelled f, /b/ spelled b, /n/ spelled n, /ŏ/ spelled o, /p/ spelled p, /th/ (voiced) spelled th, /h/ spelled h, /r/ spelled r, /ĭ/ spelled i, /f/ spelled f, /sh/ spelled sh, /ĕ/ spelled e, /d/ spelled d, /a/ spelled a, /m/ spelled m, /s/ spelled s, /t/ spelled t

High-Frequency Words Reviewed: are, the, of, is, said, and, a, to, was

Selection 41: Bump

Sound/Spelling(s) Introduced: /ŭ/ spelled u

High-Frequency Words Introduced: for, his

Selection 42: Bats!

Sound/Spelling(s) Reviewed: /ŭ/ spelled u, /g/ spelled g, /w/ spelled w_, /f/ spelled f, /b/ spelled b, /n/ spelled n, /ŏ/ spelled o, /k/ spelled c, ck; /p/ spelled p, /th/ (voiced) spelled th, /h/ spelled h, /r/ spelled r, /ĭ/ spelled i, /ĕ/ spelled e, /d/ spelled d, /a/ spelled a, /m/ spelled m, /s/ spelled s, ss; /t/ spelled t

High-Frequency Words Introduced: they

Selection 43: A Whiff!

Sound/Spelling(s) Introduced: /hw/ spelled wh

High-Frequency Words Reviewed: for, or, is, I, a, he, the, and, his, be

Selection 44: Duck Nest

Sound/Spelling(s) Introduced: /ē/ spelled ee

High-Frequency Words Reviewed: the, of, for, they, a, she, and, is, as, be

Selection 45: Bill

Sound/Spelling(s) Introduced: /l/ spelled
l, ll

High-Frequency Words Reviewed: the,
or, to, of, was, his, he, we, and, a, as, I, me

Selection 46: Sled Hill

Sound/Spelling(s) Reviewed: /hw/
spelled *wh*, /ŭ/ spelled *u*, /l/ spelled
l, ll; /b/ spelled *b*, /n/ spelled *n*, /sh/
spelled *sh*, /ō/ spelled *o*, /ŏ/ spelled *o*,
/g/ spelled *g*, /th/ (voiced) spelled *th*, /p/
spelled *p*, /h/ spelled *h*, /r/ spelled *r*, /f/
spelled *f*, /sh/ spelled *sh*, /ĭ/ spelled *i*,
/ĕ/ spelled *e*, /d/ spelled *d*, /a/ spelled
a, /m/ spelled *m*, /s/ spelled *ss, s*; /t/
spelled *t*

High-Frequency Words Reviewed: the,
was, to, of, they, be, a, is, and

Selection 47: Chet's Bench

Sound/Spelling(s) Introduced: /ch/
spelled *ch*

High-Frequency Words Introduced:
have, by

Selection 48: Cats

Sound/Spelling(s) Reviewed: /ch/
spelled *ch*, /hw/ spelled *wh*, /ŭ/ spelled
u, /l/ spelled *l, ll*; /b/ spelled *b*, /n/
spelled *n*, /ŏ/ spelled *o*, /g/ spelled
g, /w/ spelled *w_*, /p/ spelled *p*, /th/
(voiced) spelled *th*, /h/ spelled *h*, /k/

spelled *c, ck*; /r/ spelled *r*, /ĭ/ spelled *i*, /f/
spelled *f*, /ē/ spelled *ee*, /ĕ/ spelled *e*,
/d/ spelled *d*, /a/ spelled *a*, /m/ spelled
m, /s/ spelled *s, ss*; /t/ spelled *t*

High-Frequency Words Reviewed:
have, by, you, to, is, the, was, as, a, and,
or, be

Selection 49: Chet and Ann

Sound/Spelling(s) Introduced: /y/
spelled *y*

High-Frequency Words Introduced:
were

Selection 50: Yam Fests!

Sound/Spelling(s) Reviewed: /y/ spelled
y, /g/ spelled *g*, /w/ spelled *w_*; /k/
spelled *ck, c*; /b/ spelled *b*, /n/ spelled
n, /ŭ/ spelled *u*, /ō/ spelled *o*, /ŏ/
spelled *o*, /p/ spelled *p*, /l/ spelled *l, ll*;
/th/ (voiced and unvoiced) spelled *th*,
/h/ spelled *h*, /r/ spelled *r*, /ĭ/ spelled *i*, /f/
spelled *f*, /ĕ/ spelled *e*, /d/ spelled *d*, /a/
spelled *a*, /m/ spelled *m*, /s/ spelled *s*,
/t/ spelled *t*

High-Frequency Words Reviewed: by,
was, you, said, as, to, or, a, he, we, the

Selection 51: A Run

Sound/Spelling(s) Reviewed: /y/ spelled *y*, /ch/ spelled *ch*, /l/ spelled *l*, *ll*; /ŭ/ spelled *u*, /er/ spelled *er*, /p/ spelled *p*, /g/ spelled *g*, /sh/ spelled *sh*, /w/ spelled *w_*, /b/ spelled *b*, /n/ spelled *n*, /ŏ/ spelled *o*, /th/ (voiced and unvoiced) spelled *th*, /h/ spelled *h*, /r/ spelled *r*, /ĭ/ spelled *i*, /k/ spelled *ck*, /f/ spelled *f*, *ff*; /ĕ/ spelled *e*, /d/ spelled *d*, /ă/ spelled *a*, /t/ spelled *t*, /s/ spelled *s*, /m/ spelled *m*

High-Frequency Words Reviewed: the, of, by, was, were, she, a, and

Selection 52: Math

Sound/Spelling(s) Reviewed: /th/ (voiced and unvoiced) spelled *th*, /y/ spelled *y*, /g/ spelled *g*, /w/ spelled *w_*, /ch/ spelled *ch*, /k/ spelled *ck*, *c*; /h/ spelled *h*, /b/ spelled *b*, /n/ spelled *n*, /ŭ/ spelled *u*, /ō/ spelled *o*, /ŏ/ spelled *o*, /p/ spelled *p*, /l/ spelled *l*, *ll*; /th/ (voiced) spelled *th*, /r/ spelled *r*, /ĭ/ spelled *i*, /f/ spelled *f*, /ĕ/ spelled *e*, /d/ spelled *d*, /a/ spelled *a*, /m/ spelled *m*, /s/ spelled *s*, *ss*; /t/ spelled *t*

High-Frequency Words Reviewed: you, have, to, a, for, by, the, or, is, of

Selection 53: A Camp Kit

Sound/Spelling(s) Introduced: /k/ spelled *k*

High-Frequency Words Introduced: one, their, what

Selection 54: Plants That Kill

Sound/Spelling(s) Reviewed: /k/ spelled *ck, k, c*; /y/ spelled *y*, /g/ spelled *g*, /w/ spelled *w_*, /sh/ spelled *sh*, /b/ spelled *b*, /n/ spelled *n*, /ŭ/ spelled *u*, /ŏ/ spelled *o*, /p/ spelled *p*, /l/ spelled *l*, *ll*; /th/ (voiced) spelled *th*, /r/ spelled *r*, /ĭ/ spelled *i*, /ĕ/ spelled *e*, /a/ spelled *a*, /s/ spelled *s*, /t/ spelled *t*

High-Frequency Words Reviewed: of, one, or, have, you, what, a, be, the, to, and

Selection 55: Mud

Sound/Spelling(s) Introduced: /j/ spelled *j*

High-Frequency Words Reviewed: the, said, have, one, their, is, I, we, a, she, and, of

Selection 56: Jet Pack

Sound/Spelling(s) Reviewed: /j/ spelled *j*, /k/ spelled *c, ck*; /g/ spelled *g*, /w/ spelled *w_*, /h/ spelled *h*, /b/ spelled *b*, /n/ spelled *n*, /ŭ/ spelled *u*, /ō/ spelled *o*, /ŏ/ spelled *o*, /p/ spelled *p*, /l/ spelled *l*, *ll*; /th/ (voiced and unvoiced) spelled *th*, /r/ spelled *r*, /ĭ/ spelled *i*, /f/ spelled *f*, /ĕ/ spelled *e*, /d/ spelled *d*, /a/ spelled *a*, /m/ spelled *m*, /s/ spelled *s*, /t/ spelled *t*

High-Frequency Words Reviewed: is, his, are, have, to, or, one, he, the, a, and, be

Selection 57: Red Fuzz

Sound/Spelling(s) Introduced: /z/ spelled *z, zz*

High-Frequency Words Reviewed: I, is, the, you, one, have, his, and, a, we, he, as, you

Selection 58: Buzz!

Sound/Spelling(s) Reviewed: /z/ spelled *z, zz*; /hw/ spelled *wh*, /g/ spelled *g*, /w/ spelled *w_*, /k/ spelled *c*, /b/ spelled *b*, /n/ spelled *n*, /ŭ/ spelled *u*, /ŏ/ spelled *o*, /ō/ spelled *o*, /p/ spelled *p*, /l/ spelled *l, ll*; /th/ (voiced) spelled *th*, /h/ spelled *h*, /ĭ/ spelled *i*, /f/ spelled *f*, /ĕ/ spelled *e*, /d/ spelled *d*, /a/ spelled *a*, /s/ spelled *s*, /t/ spelled *t*

High-Frequency Words Reviewed: you, what, is, by, to, one, a

Selection 59: Flat or Fat?

Sound/Spelling(s) Introduced: /ī/ spelled *i_e*

High-Frequency Words Introduced: do, would

Selection 60: Slime!

Sound/Spelling(s) Reviewed: /ī/ spelled *i_e*, /y/ spelled *y*, /g/ spelled *g*, /w/

spelled *w_*, /sh/ spelled *sh*, /k/ spelled *k, c, ck*; /h/ spelled *h*, /b/ spelled *b*, /n/ spelled *n*, /ŭ/ spelled *u*, /ŏ/ spelled *o*, /p/ spelled *p*, /l/ spelled *l, ll*; /ĭ/ spelled *i*, /f/ spelled *f*, /ē/ spelled *ee*, /ĕ/ spelled *e*, /d/ spelled *d*, /r/ spelled *r*, /m/ spelled *m*, /a/ spelled *a*, /s/ spelled *s, ss*; /t/ spelled *t*

High-Frequency Words Reviewed: would, do, is, the, you, have, a, and, of, or

Selection 61: Late for the Game

Sound/Spelling(s) Introduced: /ā/ spelled *a_e*

High-Frequency Words Reviewed: was, would, by, the, what, do, of, for, to, she, a, be

Selection 62: Snakes

Sound/Spelling(s) Reviewed: /ā/ spelled *a_e*, /ī/ spelled *i_e*, /hw/ spelled *wh*, /g/ spelled *g*, /sh/ spelled *sh*, /k/ spelled *k, c, ck*; /h/ spelled *h*, /b/ spelled *b*, /n/ spelled *n*, /ŭ/ spelled *u*, /ō/ spelled *o*, /ŏ/ spelled *o*, /p/ spelled *p*, /l/ spelled *l, ll*; /w/ spelled *w_*, /th/ (voiced) spelled *th*, /ĭ/ spelled *i*, /f/ spelled *f*, /ĕ/ spelled *e*, /d/ spelled *d*, /r/ spelled *r*, /m/ spelled *m*, /a/ spelled *a*, /s/ spelled *s, ss*; /t/ spelled *t*

High-Frequency Words Introduced: your

Selection 63: Code?

Sound/Spelling(s) Introduced: /ō/ spelled *o_e*

High-Frequency Words Reviewed: to, of, was, the, said, and, I, we, a

Selection 64: A Globe

Sound/Spelling(s) Reviewed: /ō/ spelled o, o_e; /ā/ spelled a_e, /ē/ spelled ee, /y/ spelled y, /hw/ spelled wh, /ch/ spelled ch, /g/ spelled g, /k/ spelled k, c, ck; /h/ spelled h, /b/ spelled b, /n/ spelled n, /sh/ spelled sh, /ŏ/ spelled o, /p/ spelled p, /l/ spelled l, /th/ (voiced) spelled th, /ĭ/ spelled i, /f/ spelled f, /ĕ/ spelled e, /d/ spelled d, /r/ spelled r, /m/ spelled m, /a/ spelled a, /s/ spelled s, /t/ spelled t

High-Frequency Words Reviewed: your, you, the, is, or, have, a, to, and

Selection 65: Gus

Sound/Spelling(s) Introduced: /ū/ spelled u_e

High-Frequency Words Introduced: been, who

Selection 66: Mule Trips

Sound/Spelling(s) Reviewed: /ū/ spelled u_e, /ō/ spelled o, o_e; /ā/ spelled a_e, /ī/ spelled i_e, /ē/ spelled ee, /k/ spelled k, c; /j/ spelled j, /ch/ spelled ch, /g/ spelled g, /w/ spelled w_, /h/ spelled h, /hw/ spelled wh, /b/ spelled b, /n/ spelled n, /ŭ/ spelled u, /ŏ/ spelled o, /p/ spelled p, /l/ spelled l, ll; /th/ (voiced and unvoiced) spelled th, /ĭ/ spelled i, /f/

spelled f, ff; /ĕ/ spelled e, /d/ spelled d, /r/ spelled r, /m/ spelled m, /a/ spelled a, /s/ spelled s, /t/ spelled t

High-Frequency Words Reviewed: who, has, been, is, the, are, or, you, to, by, your, would, a, I, was, he, she, of, his, and, be

Selection 67: Dave and Vick

Sound/Spelling(s) Introduced: /v/ spelled v

High-Frequency Words Introduced: my, new, very

Selection 68: Cave Life

Sound/Spelling(s) Reviewed: /v/ spelled v, /ā/ spelled a_e, /ī/ spelled i_e, /ē/ spelled ee, /ō/ spelled o_e, /sh/ spelled sh, /k/ spelled k, c, ck; /ŭ/ spelled u, /er/ spelled er, /ŏ/ spelled o, /p/ spelled p, /n/ spelled n, /b/ spelled b, /g/ spelled g, /l/ spelled l, ll; /th/ (voiced) spelled th, /h/ spelled h, /w/ spelled w_, /ch/ spelled ch, /hw/ spelled wh, /ĭ/ spelled i, /f/ spelled f, /ĕ/ spelled e, /d/ spelled d, dd; /r/ spelled r, /m/ spelled m, /a/ spelled a, /s/ spelled s, ss; /t/ spelled t

High-Frequency Words Reviewed: they, to, the, very, do, of, a, or, and, is, be

Selection 69: Fox Lake

Sound/Spelling(s) Introduced: /ks/ spelled x

High-Frequency Words Introduced:
may, these, where

Selection 70: Red Fox

Sound/Spelling(s) Reviewed: /ks/
spelled x, /v/ spelled v, /ō/ spelled o,
o_e; /ī/ spelled i_e, /ā/ spelled a_e,
/hw/ spelled wh, /g/ spelled g, /ē/
spelled ee, /w/ spelled w_, /sh/ spelled
sh, /h/ spelled h, /k/ spelled k, c, ck; /b/
spelled b, /n/ spelled n, /ŭ/ spelled u,
/er/ spelled er, /ŏ/ spelled o, /p/ spelled
p, /l/ spelled l, ll; /th/ (voiced) spelled th,
/ĭ/ spelled i, /f/ spelled f, /ĕ/ spelled e,
/d/ spelled d, /r/ spelled r, /m/ spelled m,
/a/ spelled a, /s/ spelled s, /t/ spelled t

High-Frequency Words Reviewed: or,
have, of, the, to, you, new, your, do, a,
be, very, where, are, and, for, may, these

Selection 71: Read! Read! Read!

Sound/Spelling(s) Introduced: /ē/
spelled ea

High-Frequency Words Reviewed: you,
the, your, what, where, or, may, they, to,
these, be, a, and, is

Selection 72: A Beach

Sound/Spelling(s) Reviewed: /ē/ spelled
e, ee, ea; /v/ spelled v, /ō/ spelled o,
o_e; /ā/ spelled a_e, /ī/ spelled i_e,
/j/ spelled j, /k/ spelled k, c, ck; /hw/
spelled wh, /sh/ spelled sh, /g/ spelled

g, /w/ spelled w_, /h/ spelled h, /b/
spelled b, /n/ spelled n, /ŭ/ spelled u, /ŏ/
spelled o, /p/ spelled p, /l/ spelled l, ll;
/ch/ spelled ch, /th/ (voiced) spelled th,
/ĭ/ spelled i, /f/ spelled f, /ĕ/ spelled e, /d/
spelled d, /r/ spelled r, /m/ spelled m, /a/
spelled a, /s/ spelled s, ss; /t/ spelled t

High-Frequency Words Reviewed: the,
you, is, or, do, of, are, these, where,
have, may, to, a, and, what, they, be

Selection 73: Drive!

Sound/Spelling(s) Introduced: /or/
spelled or, /ar/ spelled ar

High-Frequency Words Reviewed: was,
his, I, the, by, one, to, where, said, as, a,
or, he, me, we, and, your, you, be

Selection 74: Farm Park

Sound/Spelling(s) Reviewed: /or/ spelled
or, /ar/ spelled ar, /ē/ spelled ee, ea;
/ō/ spelled o, o_e; /ā/ spelled a_e, /ī/
spelled i_e, /y/ spelled y, /k/ spelled
c, k, ck; /hw/ spelled wh, /ch/ spelled
ch, /g/ spelled g, /w/ spelled w_, /sh/
spelled sh, /h/ spelled h, /b/ spelled b,
/n/ spelled n, /ŭ/ spelled u, /ŏ/ spelled o,
/p/ spelled p, /l/ spelled l, ll; /th/ (voiced)
spelled th, /ĭ/ spelled i, /f/ spelled f, /ĕ/
spelled e, /d/ spelled d, /r/ spelled r, /m/
spelled m, /a/ spelled a, /s/ spelled s,
ss; /t/ spelled t

High-Frequency Words Reviewed: was, my, I, would, the, is, to, has, you, where, your, may, a, we, and, be

Selection 75: At Bat

Sound/Spelling(s) Introduced: /ur/ spelled *ir*; /ur/ spelled *ur*

High-Frequency Words Introduced: long, only, two

Selection 76: White Shark

Sound/Spelling(s) Introduced: /ur/ spelled *ir, ur*; /or/ spelled *or*, /ar/ spelled *ar*, /ā/ spelled *a_e*, /ē/ spelled *ee, ea*; /v/ spelled *v*, /ī/ spelled *i_e*, /j/ spelled *j*, /k/ spelled *c, k, ck*; /hw/ spelled *wh*, /ch/ spelled *ch*, /g/ spelled *g*, /w/ spelled *w_*, /h/ spelled *h*, /b/ spelled *b*, /n/ spelled *n*, /ŭ/ spelled *u*, /ŏ/ spelled *o*, /p/ spelled *p*, /l/ spelled *l, ll*; /sh/ spelled *sh*, /th/ (voiced and unvoiced) spelled *th*, /ĭ/ spelled *i*, /f/ spelled *f*, /ĕ/ spelled *e*, /d/ spelled *d*, /r/ spelled *r*, /m/ spelled *m*, /a/ spelled *a*, /s/ spelled *s*, /t/ spelled *t*

High-Frequency Words Reviewed: of, what, the, long, only, two, to, do, you, a, and, or, may, has

Selection 77: Cents

Sound/Spelling(s) Introduced: /s/ spelled *ce, ci*

High-Frequency Words Introduced: also, now, down

Selection 78: Not Mice!

Sound/Spelling(s) Reviewed: /s/ spelled *ce, ci, s*; /or/ spelled *or*, /ar/ spelled *ar*, /ks/ spelled *x*, /z/ spelled *z*, /ē/ spelled *ee, ea*; /ā/ spelled *a_e*, /ī/ spelled *i_e*, /y/ spelled *y*, /k/ spelled *c, k*; /g/ spelled *g*, /w/ spelled *w_*, /h/ spelled *h*, /b/ spelled *b*, /n/ spelled *n*, /ō/ spelled *o*, *o_e*; /ŏ/ spelled *o*, /ŭ/ spelled *u*, /er/ spelled *er*, /p/ spelled *p*, /l/ spelled *l, ll*; /ch/ spelled *ch*, /th/ (voiced and unvoiced) spelled *th*; /ĭ/ spelled *i*, /f/ spelled *f, ff*; /ĕ/ spelled *e*, /d/ spelled *d*, /r/ spelled *r*, /m/ spelled *m*, /a/ spelled *a*, /t/ spelled *t*

High-Frequency Words Reviewed: are, or, to, we, do, a, and, they, of, long, the, what, these, only

Selection 79: A Big Barn Fire!

Sound/Spelling(s) Introduced: /oo/ spelled *oo (moon)*

High-Frequency Words Introduced: called, know, through

Selection 80: A Loon

Sound/Spelling(s) Reviewed: /oo/ spelled *oo (moon)*, /ur/ spelled *ir*, /or/ spelled *or*, /ē/ spelled *ee, ea*; /v/ spelled *v*, /ī/ spelled *i_e*, /ā/ spelled *a_e*, /k/ spelled *k, c, ck*; /hw/ spelled *wh*, /ch/ spelled *ch*, /g/ spelled *g*, /w/ spelled *w_*, /h/ spelled *h*, /b/ spelled *b*, /n/ spelled *n*, /ŭ/ spelled *u*, /ŏ/ spelled *o*,

/p/ spelled *p*, /l/ spelled *l, ll*; /z/ spelled *z*, /sh/ spelled *sh*, /th/ (voiced and unvoiced) spelled *th*, /ĭ/ spelled *i*, /f/ spelled *f*, /ĕ/ spelled *e*, /d/ spelled *d, dd*; /r/ spelled *r*, /m/ spelled *m*, /a/ spelled *a*, /s/ spelled *s*, /t/ spelled *t*

High-Frequency Words Reviewed: called, know, through, do, you, what, is, as, long, has, have, one, a, or, be, for, and

Selection 81: A Bike Ride

Sound/Spelling(s) Introduced: /ō/ spelled *oa*

High-Frequency Words Reviewed: called, know, through, do, to, said, you, would, is, have, one, a, we, he, of, and, I

Selection 82: Do Goats Eat Tin?

Sound/Spelling(s) Reviewed: /ō/ spelled *oa*, /or/ spelled *or*, /ar/ spelled *ar*, /ē/ spelled *ee, ea*; /ī/ spelled *i_e*, /ā/ spelled *a_e*, /k/ spelled *k, c, ck*; /hw/ spelled *wh*, /g/ spelled *g*, /w/ spelled *w_*, /ch/ spelled *ch*, /b/ spelled *b*, /n/ spelled *n*, /ŏ/ spelled *o*, /ŭ/ spelled *u*, /p/ spelled *p*, /l/ spelled *l, ll*; /th/ (voiced) spelled *th*, /ĭ/ spelled *i*, /f/ spelled *f, ff*; /ĕ/ spelled *e*, /d/ spelled *d, dd*; /r/ spelled *r*, /m/ spelled *m*, /a/ spelled *a*, /s/ spelled *s, ss*; /t/ spelled *t*

High-Frequency Words Reviewed: do, is, of, your, they, know, through, a, or, and, as, be, the, to, what, these

Selection 83: Quack

Sound/Spelling(s) Introduced: /kw/ spelled *qu_*

High-Frequency Words Reviewed: was, the, through, called, you, to, as, of, know, said, his, he, a, and, I

Selection 84: Quilt Art

Sound/Spelling(s) Introduced: /air/ spelled *are*

High-Frequency Words Reviewed: do, you, have, called, one, the, to, of, a, be, or, as, and, for

Selection 85: Fred's

Sound/Spelling(s) Introduced: /z/ spelled *s*

High-Frequency Words Introduced: little, why

Selection 86: Dart Frogs

Sound/Spelling(s) Reviewed: /z/ spelled *s, z*; /ur/ spelled *ir*, /oo/ spelled *oo* (moon), /or/ spelled *or*, /ar/ spelled *ar*, /ē/ spelled *ee, ea*; /ī/ spelled *i_e*, /j/ spelled *j*, /ā/ spelled *a_e*, /ū/ spelled *u_e*, /ō/ spelled *o*, /k/ spelled *k, c, ck*; /y/ spelled *y*, /hw/ spelled *wh*, /v/ spelled *v*, /g/ spelled *g*, /ch/ spelled *ch*, /w/ spelled *w_*, /h/ spelled *h*, /b/ spelled *b*, /n/ spelled *n*, /ŏ/ spelled *o*, /ŭ/ spelled *u*, /p/ spelled *p*, /l/ spelled *l, ll*; /sh/ spelled *sh*, /th/ (voiced) spelled *th*, /ĭ/ spelled *i*,

/f/ spelled *f*, /ĕ/ spelled *e*, /d/ spelled *d*, /r/ spelled *r*, /a/ spelled *a*, /m/ spelled *m*, /s/ spelled *s, ss, ce*; /t/ spelled *t*

High-Frequency Words Reviewed: are, little, their, of, to, do, you, they, know, these, or, and, is, for, why, a, one

Selection 87: My Job

Sound/Spelling(s) Introduced: (/ā/) spelled *ai, ay*

High-Frequency Words Reviewed: my, you, the, why, are, their, to, one, was, little, do, have, is, these, and, I, may, a, we

Selection 88: Slime

Sound/Spelling(s) Reviewed: /ā/ spelled *ai, ay, a_e*; /z/ spelled *s, z*; /ō/ spelled *oa*, /oo/ spelled *oo (moon)*, /s/ spelled *ce, s*; /ur/ spelled *ir*, /or/ spelled *or*, /ar/ spelled *ar*, /ē/ spelled *ee, ea*; /ī/ spelled *i_e*, /y/ spelled *y*, /k/ spelled *c, k, ck*; /hw/ spelled *wh*, /v/ spelled *v*, /g/ spelled *g*, /w/ spelled *w_*, /h/ spelled *h*, /b/ spelled *b*, /n/ spelled *n*, /ŏ/ spelled *o*, /ū/ spelled *u*, /p/ spelled *p*, /l/ spelled *l, ll*; /sh/ spelled *sh*, /th/ (voiced and unvoiced) spelled *th*, /y/ spelled *y*, /ĭ/ spelled *i*, /f/ spelled *f, ff*; /ĕ/ spelled *e*, /d/ spelled *d*, /r/ spelled *r*, /m/ spelled *m*, /a/ spelled *a*, /t/ spelled *t*

High-Frequency Words Reviewed: what, the, little, you, to, do, why, a, and, is, as, or, has

Selection 89: Dreams

Sound/Spelling(s) Introduced: /ī/ spelled *i, igh, ie, y*

High-Frequency Words Introduced: good, work, any

Selection 90: A Drone

Sound/Spelling(s) Reviewed: /ī/ spelled *i, igh, ie, y, i_e*; /s/ spelled *ce, s*; /ē/ spelled *ee, ea*; /ō/ spelled *o_e*, /ā/ spelled *a_e*, /j/ spelled *j*, /k/ spelled *k, c, ck*; /g/ spelled *g*, /ch/ spelled *ch*, /w/ spelled *w_*, /z/ spelled *s*, /ks/ spelled *x*, /h/ spelled *h*, /b/ spelled *b*, /n/ spelled *n*, /ŏ/ spelled *o*, /ū/ spelled *u*, /p/ spelled *p*, /l/ spelled *l*, /th/ (voiced and unvoiced) spelled *th*, /ĭ/ spelled *i*, /f/ spelled *f*, /ĕ/ spelled *e*, /d/ spelled *d*, /r/ spelled *r*, /m/ spelled *m*, /a/ spelled *a*, /t/ spelled *t*

High-Frequency Words Reviewed: good, work, any, the, little, to, you, who, through, what, a, is, he, his, by, has, of

Selection 91: Fair!

Sound/Spelling(s) Introduced: /ā/ spelled *a*

High-Frequency Words Reviewed: good, work, any, the, to, was, two, of, for, and, I, a, we, me, were, my

Selection 92: Jets!

Sound/Spelling(s) Reviewed: /ā/ spelled *ai, ay, a_e;* /a/ spelled *a,* /kw/ spelled *qu,* /ō/ spelled *o, o_e;* /ur/ spelled *ur,* /oo/ spelled *oo (moon),* /ē/ spelled *ee, ea;* /ī/ spelled *i_e, ie;* /y/ spelled *y,* /ks/ spelled *x,* /k/ spelled *k, c, ck;* /j/ spelled *j,* /z/ spelled *z, s;* /hw/ spelled *wh,* /v/ spelled *v,* /ch/ spelled *ch,* /g/ spelled *g,* /w/ spelled *w_,* /b/ spelled *b,* /n/ spelled *n,* /er/ spelled *er,* /ū/ spelled *u,* /ŏ/ spelled *o,* /p/ spelled *p,* /l/ spelled *l, ll;* /sh/ spelled *sh,* /th/ (voiced and unvoiced) spelled *th,* /ĭ/ spelled *i,* /f/ spelled *f,* /ĕ/ spelled *e,* /d/ spelled *d,* /r/ spelled *r,* /m/ spelled *m,* /s/ spelled *s,* /t/ spelled *t*

High-Frequency Words Reviewed: they, the, who, are, of, one, two, to, good, and, a, be

Selection 93: Stairs

Sound/Spelling(s) Introduced: /air/ spelled *air*

High-Frequency Words Reviewed: to, the, one, said, work, they, of, any, we, his, I, by, and, a, was, is

Selection 94: Night Lights

Sound/Spelling(s) Reviewed: /air/ spelled *air, are;* /ā/ spelled *ai, a_e;* /z/ spelled *s,* /ē/ spelled *ee, ea;* /ī/ spelled *igh, ie, y, i_e;* /k/ spelled *k,* /hw/ spelled *wh,* /g/ spelled *g,* /ch/ spelled *ch,* /h/ spelled *h,* /b/ spelled *b,* /n/ spelled *n,* /ŭ/

spelled *u,* /ŏ/ spelled *o,* /p/ spelled *p,* /l/ spelled *l, ll;* /sh/ spelled *sh,* /th/ (voiced) spelled *th,* /ĭ/ spelled *i,* /f/ spelled *f,* /ĕ/ spelled *e,* /d/ spelled *d,* /r/ spelled *r,* /m/ spelled *m,* /a/ spelled *a,* /s/ spelled *s, ce;* /t/ spelled *t*

High-Frequency Words Reviewed: the, of, they, what, were, do, good, work, are, their, we, a, for, these, is, as, and

Selection 95: A Gray Ship

Sound/Spelling(s) Introduced: /j/ spelled *ge, dge*

High-Frequency Words Introduced: come, should, things

Selection 96: Hard Work

Sound/Spelling(s) Reviewed: /ū/ spelled *u_e,* /j/ spelled *j, ge, dge;* /ā/ spelled *a_e, ai;* /ō/ spelled *o, oa, o_e;* /or/ spelled *or,* /ar/ spelled *ar,* /ē/ spelled *ee, ea;* /ī/ spelled *i_e,* /k/ spelled *k, c, ck;* /v/ spelled *v,* /g/ spelled *g,* /ch/ spelled *ch,* /ks/ spelled *x,* /z/ spelled *s,* /h/ spelled *h,* /b/ spelled *b,* /n/ spelled *n,* /ŭ/ spelled *u,* /ŏ/ spelled *o,* /p/ spelled *p,* /l/ spelled *l,* /sh/ spelled *sh,* /th/ (voiced) spelled *th,* /ĭ/ spelled *i,* /f/ spelled *f,* /ĕ/ spelled *e,* /d/ spelled *d,* /r/ spelled *r,* /m/ spelled *m,* /a/ spelled *a,* /s/ spelled *s,* /t/ spelled *t*

High-Frequency Words Reviewed: long, to, there, come, they, the, of, things, are, who, where, should, work, is, a, as, has, and, or, be, he, any

Selection 97: At Sea

Sound/Spelling(s) Introduced: /ū/ spelled *u*

High-Frequency Words Reviewed: their, little, have, the, was, would, come, should, said, been, they, to, things, of, now, know, through, one, who, two, were, and, a, we, may, as, very, these, is

Selection 98: Play Music!

Sound/Spelling(s) Reviewed: /ū/ spelled *u*, /ŭ/ spelled *u*, /j/ spelled *ge*, /ī/ spelled *igh*, /ā/ spelled *ay, a_e*; /or/ spelled *or*, /ar/ spelled *ar*, /ē/ spelled *ea*, /k/ spelled *c*, k; /v/ spelled *v*, /g/ spelled *g*, /w/ spelled *w_*, /ch/ spelled *ch*, /ks/ spelled *x*, /z/ spelled *s*, /h/ spelled *h*, /b/ spelled *b*, /n/ spelled *n*, /er/ spelled *er*, /ŏ/ spelled *o*, /p/ spelled *p*, /l/ spelled *l*, *ll*; /th/ (voiced and unvoiced) spelled *th*, /ĭ/ spelled *i*, /f/ spelled *f*, /ĕ/ spelled *e*, /d/ spelled *d*, /r/ spelled *r*, /m/ spelled *m*, /a/ spelled *a*, /s/ spelled *s*, *ss*; /t/ spelled *t*

High-Frequency Words Reviewed: are, you, to, works, should, a, or, be, the, we, and, of, know

Selection 99: Mitch

Sound/Spelling(s) Introduced: /ch/ spelled *tch*

High-Frequency Words Introduced: another, around, away

Selection 100: A Hen Egg

Sound/Spelling(s) Introduced: /ō/ spelled *ow*

High-Frequency Words Reviewed: another, around, away, the, to, a, has, and, long, work, be, as, is

Selection 101: Gramps

Sound/Spelling(s) Introduced: /oo/ spelled *ew*

High-Frequency Words Reviewed: was, around, said, are, of, what, little, do, you, another, through, the, his, he, a, I, as, me, these, is, and, new, by, my

Selection 102: Fire!

Sound/Spelling(s) Reviewed: /oo/ spelled *ew*, /ch/ spelled *ch, tch*; /ū/ spelled *u, u_e*; /j/ spelled *j, ge*; /ā/ spelled *a_e, ay*; /z/ spelled *s*, /ur/ spelled *ur*, /or/ spelled *or*, /ar/ spelled *ar*, /ō/ spelled *o_e, oa*; /oo/ spelled *oo* (moon), /ē/ spelled *ee*, /ī/ spelled *i_e, igh, y*; /y/ spelled *y*, /k/ spelled *c, k, ck*; /g/ spelled *g*, /ch/ spelled *tch, ch*; /w/ spelled *w_*, /h/ spelled *h*, /b/ spelled *b*, /n/ spelled *n*, /ŭ/ spelled *u*, /ŏ/ spelled *o*, /p/ spelled *p*, /l/ spelled *l*, *ll*; /sh/ spelled *sh*, /th/ (voiced and unvoiced) spelled *th*, /ĭ/ spelled *i*, /f/ spelled *f*, /ĕ/ spelled *e*, /d/ spelled *d*, /r/ spelled *r*, /m/ spelled m, /a/ spelled *a*, /s/ spelled *s*, /t/ spelled *t*

High-Frequency Words Reviewed:
the, were, around, to, was, one, they,
another, of, little, away, a, what, should,
and, be, for, would, long, as

Selection 103: Paws?

Sound/Spelling(s) Introduced: /aw/
spelled aw

High-Frequency Words Reviewed: the,
was, were, would, of, around, away,
what, to, said, they, do, good, a, and, I,
as, or, me, my

Selection 104: Bobcats

Sound/Spelling(s) Reviewed: /aw/
spelled aw, /oo/ spelled ew, /ū/ spelled
u, /j/ spelled j, /ā/ spelled a_e, ay; /z/
spelled s, /or/ spelled or, /oo/ spelled
oo (moon), /ur/ spelled ir, /ē/ spelled ee,
ea; /ī/ spelled i_e, igh; /k/ spelled c, k,
ck; /hw/ spelled wh, /g/ spelled g, /w/
spelled w_, /h/ spelled h, /b/ spelled b,
/n/ spelled n, /ū/ spelled u, /er/ spelled
er, /ō/ spelled o, /ŏ/ spelled o, /p/
spelled p, /l/ spelled l, ll; /th/ (voiced
and unvoiced) spelled th, /ĭ/ spelled i, /f/
spelled f, /ĕ/ spelled e, /d/ spelled d, /r/
spelled r, /m/ spelled m, /a/ spelled a,
/s/ spelled s, ce; /t/ spelled t

High-Frequency Words Reviewed: do,
around, your, you, long, are, to, the, a,
is, as, may, and, down

Selection 105: Snow

Sound/Spelling(s) Reviewed: /z/ spelled
s, /ur/ spelled ir, /or/ spelled or, /ē/
spelled ea, /ā/ spelled a_e, ay; /ī/
spelled i_e, /j/ spelled j, /y/ spelled y, /l/
spelled l, ll; /er/ spelled er, /p/ spelled
p, /ō/ spelled o, o_e, oa, ow; /g/ spelled
g, /sh/ spelled sh, /w/ spelled w_, /b/
spelled b, /n/ spelled n, /ŏ/ spelled o,
/th/ (voiced and unvoiced) spelled th,
/h/ spelled h, /r/ spelled r, /ī/ spelled i,
/k/ spelled c,k; /f/ spelled f, /ĕ/ spelled
e, /d/ spelled d, /a/ spelled a, /t/ spelled
t, /s/ spelled s, ss; /m/ spelled m

High-Frequency Words Introduced:
found, known, off

Selection 106: Fish That Glow

Sound/Spelling(s) Reviewed: /ō/
spelled o, o_e, ow; /oo/ spelled ew,
oo (moon), /ch/ spelled ch, tch; /j/
spelled j, /ā/ spelled ay, /z/ spelled
s, /or/ spelled or, /ar/ spelled ar, /ē/
spelled ee, ea; /ī/ spelled i_e, igh; /k/
spelled k, c, ck; /hw/ spelled wh, /g/
spelled g, /w/ spelled w_, /h/ spelled
h, /b/ spelled b, /n/ spelled n, /ū/
spelled u, /ŏ/ spelled o, /p/ spelled p,
/l/ spelled l, ll; /th/ (voiced) spelled th,
/sh/ spelled sh, /ī/ spelled i, /f/ spelled
f, ff; /ĕ/ spelled e, /d/ spelled d, /r/
spelled r, /m/ spelled m, /a/ spelled a,
/s/ spelled s, /t/ spelled t

High-Frequency Words Reviewed: they,
are, found, of, the, would, to, another,

away, one, you, little, a, is, be, we, know, why, and, off, or, known

Selection 107: Toy Drive

Sound/Spelling(s) Introduced: /oy/ spelled *oy*

High-Frequency Words Reviewed: the, was, who, have, to, would, off, said, they, of, found, a, for, and, these, we, he, I, know, do, known

Selection 108: Soy

Sound/Spelling(s) Reviewed: /oy/ spelled *oy*, /ur/ spelled *ir*, /ō/ spelled *ow, o*; /ū/ spelled *u*, /j/ spelled *j*, /ā/ spelled *ai, ay, a_e*; /z/ spelled *s*, /ks/ spelled *x*, /or/ spelled *or*, /ar/ spelled *ar*, /oo/ spelled *oo (moon)*, /ē/ spelled *ee, ea*; /v/ spelled *v*, /ī/ spelled *i_e, igh*; /k/ spelled *c, k, ck*; /g/ spelled *g*, /ch/ spelled *ch*, /w/ spelled *w_*, /h/ spelled *h*, /b/ spelled *b*, /n/ spelled *n*, /ŭ/ spelled *u*, /p/ spelled *p*, /ŏ/ spelled *o*, /l/ spelled *l, ll*; /th/ (voiced and unvoiced) spelled *th*, /sh/ spelled *sh*, /s/ spelled *s, ce*; /ĭ/ spelled *i*, /f/ spelled *f*, /ĕ/ spelled *e*, /d/ spelled *d*, /r/ spelled *r*, /m/ spelled *m*, /a/ spelled *a*, /t/ spelled *t*

High-Frequency Words Reviewed: you, they, of, your, away, know, another, do, around, as, are, and, is, a, one, or, be, little, we, the, for, may

Selection 109: The Best Sauce

Sound/Spelling(s) Introduced: /aw/ spelled *au*

High-Frequency Words Reviewed: said, to, the, work, what, of, off, good, one, do, is, my, a, known, as, know, I, be

Selection 110: Quakes

Sound/Spelling(s) Reviewed: /aw/ spelled *au*, /ō/ spelled *o_e, ow*; /kw/ spelled *qu_*, /j/ spelled *ge*, /ā/ spelled *a_e*, /ar/ spelled *ar*, /ē/ spelled *ee, ea*; /v/ spelled *v*, /ī/ spelled *i_e, igh*; /k/ spelled *c, ck, k*; /z/ spelled *s*, /g/ spelled *g*, /w/ spelled *w_*, /h/ spelled *h*, /b/ spelled *b*, /n/ spelled *n*, /ū/ spelled *u*, /ŏ/ spelled *o*, /p/ spelled *p*, /l/ spelled *l, ll*; /th/ (voiced) spelled *th*, /sh/ spelled *sh*, /ĭ/ spelled *i*, /f/ spelled *f*, /ĕ/ spelled *e*, /d/ spelled *d*, /r/ spelled *r*, /m/ spelled *m*, /a/ spelled *a*, /s/ spelled *s, ss*; /t/ spelled *t*

High-Frequency Words Reviewed: have, you, your, what, long, known, the, through, are, of, where, they, a, or, for, we, these, is, has, as, another, and, one

Selection 111: Tess

Sound/Spelling(s) Introduced: /al/ spelled *al*

High-Frequency Words Introduced: every, put, thought

Selection 112: Green Walls

Sound/Spelling(s) Reviewed: /al/ spelled *al*, /ō/ spelled *o_e, ow*; /ū/ spelled *u*, /y/ spelled *y*, /j/ spelled *j*, /ā/ spelled *a_e, ay*; /air/ spelled *air*, /ar/ spelled *ar*, /oo/ spelled *oo (moon)*, /ē/ spelled *ee, ea*; /v/ spelled *v*, /ī/ spelled *i_e, igh*; /k/ spelled *k, c, ck*; /z/ spelled *s*, /hw/ spelled *wh*, /g/ spelled *g*, /ch/ spelled *ch*, /w/ spelled *w_*, /h/ spelled *h*, /sh/ spelled *sh*, /b/ spelled *b*, /n/ spelled *n*, /ŭ/ spelled *u*, /ŏ/ spelled *o*, /p/ spelled *p*, /l/ spelled *l, ll*; /th/ (voiced and unvoiced) spelled *th*, /s/ spelled *s, ss, ce*; /ĭ/ spelled *i*, /f/ spelled *f*, /ĕ/ spelled *e*, /d/ spelled *d*, /r/ spelled *r*, /m/ spelled *m*, /a/ spelled *a*, /t/ spelled *t*

High-Frequency Words Reviewed: every, put, thought, have, you, of, do, the, they, good, one, these, be, and, or, a, why, we, as, is, for, to

Selection 113: Chimes

Sound/Spelling(s) Introduced: /ow/ spelled *ou (loud)*

High-Frequency Words Reviewed: every, would, the, was, they, put, one, thought, by, to, a, good, or, he, and, new

Selection 114: Just a Little Rain?

Sound/Spelling(s) Reviewed: /ow/ spelled *ou (loud)*, /al/ spelled *al*, /air/ spelled *air*, /ō/ spelled *o_e, oa*; /ū/ spelled *u*, /j/ spelled *j*, /ā/ spelled *a_e, ai, ay*; /or/ spelled *or*, /oo/ spelled *oo*

(moon), /ē/ spelled *ee*, /ī/ spelled *ie, igh, i_e*; /v/ spelled *v*, /k/ spelled *k*, /z/ spelled *s, z*; /ch/ spelled *ch*, /g/ spelled *g*, /w/ spelled *w_*, /h/ spelled *h*, /sh/ spelled *sh*, /b/ spelled *b*, /n/ spelled *n*, /ŭ/ spelled *u*, /ŏ/ spelled *o*, /p/ spelled *p*, /l/ spelled *l, ll*; /th/ (voiced and unvoiced) spelled *th*, /s/ spelled *ce, s, ss*; /ī/ spelled *i*, /f/ spelled *f*, /ĕ/ spelled *e*, /d/ spelled *d*, /r/ spelled *r*, /m/ spelled *m*, /a/ spelled *a*, /t/ spelled *t*

High-Frequency Words Reviewed: every, would, any, the, put, do, to, long, we, and, may, a, or, for, by, is, found, of, little

Selection 115: Cold?

Sound/Spelling(s) Introduced: (/m/) spelled *mb*

High-Frequency Words Reviewed: the, thing, to, puts, you, a, he, I, is, his, and, now, we, for

Selection 116: Thumbs

Sound/Spelling(s) Reviewed: /m/ spelled *mb, m*; /al/ spelled *al*, /ū/ spelled *u_e*, /ō/ spelled *o_e, ow, o*; /ā/ spelled *a_e*, /air/ spelled *air*, /or/ spelled *or*, /ar/ spelled *ar*, /er/ spelled *er*, /ē/ spelled *e, ee, ea*; /v/ spelled *v*, /ī/ spelled *i_e, i, igh*; /k/ spelled *k, c, ck*; /z/ spelled *s*, /s/ spelled *s, ce*; /hw/ spelled *wh*, /g/ spelled *g*, /w/ spelled *w_*, /sh/ spelled *sh*, /h/ spelled *h*, /b/ spelled *b*, /n/ spelled *n*, /ŭ/ spelled *u*, /ŏ/ spelled *o*, /p/ spelled *p*, /l/ spelled *l, ll*; /th/ (voiced and unvoiced) spelled *th*,

/ĭ/ spelled *i*, /y/ spelled *y*, /f/ spelled *f*, /ĕ/ spelled *e*, /d/ spelled *d, dd;* /r/ spelled *r*, /a/ spelled *a*, /t/ spelled *t*

High-Frequency Words Reviewed: the, you, have, should, your, every, do, things, to, thought, what, said, we, I, a, and, may, my, know, me, new, down

Selection 117: What Kate Knows

Sound/Spelling(s) Introduced: /n/ spelled *kn*

High-Frequency Words Introduced: again, although, once

Selection 118: Storm!

Sound/Spelling(s) Reviewed: /n/ spelled *kn, n;* /ow/ spelled *ou (loud)*, /ur/ spelled *ur*, /ō/ spelled *ow*, /ā/ spelled *ay, a_e;* /or/ spelled *or*, /ar/ spelled *ar*, /v/ spelled *v*, /ē/ spelled *e, ee;* /ī/ spelled *i_e, ie, igh;* /j/ spelled *ge*, /y/ spelled *y*, /k/ spelled *c, k, ck;* /hw/ spelled *wh*, /g/ spelled *g*, /ch/ spelled *tch*, /w/ spelled *w_*, /z/ spelled *s*, /sh/ spelled *sh*, /h/ spelled *h*, /b/ spelled *b*, /ŏ/ spelled *o*, /ŭ/ spelled *u*, /p/ spelled *p*, /l/ spelled *l, ll;* /th/ (voiced and unvoiced) spelled *th*, /s/ spelled *s, ss, ce;* /ĭ/ spelled *i*, /f/ spelled *f*, /ĕ/ spelled *e*, /d/ spelled *d*, /r/ spelled *r*, /m/ spelled *m*, /a/ spelled *a*, /t/ spelled *t*

High-Frequency Words Reviewed: although, again, once, to, you, your, are,

things, were, away, a, be, know, the, or, may, be, as, is, has, of

Selection 119: Look!

Sound/Spelling(s) Introduced: /oo/ spelled *oo (took)*

High-Frequency Words Reviewed: although, again, once, the, they, what, you, said, to, were, and, by, a, his, or, know, as, good, be, down, is, she, off

Selection 120: Sod Homes

Sound/Spelling(s) Reviewed: /oo/ spelled *oo (took), oo (moon);* /al/ spelled *al*, /are/ spelled *are*, /aw/ spelled *aw*, /ow/ spelled *ou (loud)*, /al/ spelled *al*, /ow/ spelled *ow*, /ks/ spelled *x*, /ā/ spelled *a_e*, /kw/ spelled *qu*, /or/ spelled *or*, /ur/ spelled *ir*, /ar/ spelled *ar*, /ē/ spelled *e, ee;* /ī/ spelled *i_e, i, igh;* /k/ spelled *c, k, ck;* /g/ spelled *g*, /w/ spelled *w_*, /h/ spelled *h*, /b/ spelled *b*, /n/ spelled *n*, /ŭ/ spelled *u*, /ō/ spelled *o, o_e;* /ŏ/ spelled *o*, /p/ spelled *p*, /l/ spelled *l, ll;* /th/ (voiced and unvoiced) spelled *th*, /s/ spelled *s, ss, ce;* /z/ spelled *s*, /ĭ/ spelled *i*, /f/ spelled *f*, /ĕ/ spelled *e*, /d/ spelled *d*, /r/ spelled *r*, /m/ spelled *m*, /a/ spelled *a*, /t/ spelled *t*

High-Frequency Words Reviewed: although, again, the, was, to, were, of, you, have, once, would, a, good, be, and, is, or

Selection 121: Go to Seed?

Sound/Spelling(s) Introduced: /f/ spelled *ph*

High-Frequency Words Reviewed: do, you, the, to, of, one, once, two, again, they, know, things, a, has, and, why, we, or, new, is

Selection 122: Phones

Sound/Spelling(s) Reviewed: /f/ spelled *ph, f;* /oo/ spelled *oo (took), ew;* /ow/ spelled *ou (loud),* /v/ spelled *v,* /ō/ spelled *o_e, ow;* /al/ spelled *al,* /or/ spelled *or,* /ar/ spelled *ar,* /ē/ spelled *ea, ee, y;* /ī/ spelled *i, igh, i_e;* /ā/ spelled *a_e,* /ū/ spelled *u_e,* /k/ spelled *c, k, ck;* /g/ spelled *g,* /ch/ spelled *ch,* /w/ spelled *w_,* /h/ spelled *h,* /b/ spelled *b,* /n/ spelled *n, kn;* /ŏ/ spelled *o,* /ch/ spelled *ch,* /ŭ/ spelled *u,* /p/ spelled *p,* /l/ spelled *l, ll;* /th/ (voiced) spelled *th,* /s/ spelled *s, ss, ce;* /z/ spelled *s,* /ĭ/ spelled *i,* /f/ spelled *f,* /ĕ/ spelled *e,* /d/ spelled *d,* /r/ spelled *r,* /m/ spelled *m,* /a/ spelled *a,* /t/ spelled *t*

High-Frequency Words Reviewed: do, you, have, were, they, would, through, everywhere, once, around, although, only, a, the, known, as, these, I, and, be, to, off, work, now, we, are

Selection 123: Wilbur and Orville

Sound/Spelling(s) Introduced: /r/ spelled *wr*

High-Frequency Words Introduced: does, enough, taught

Selection 124: Flight

Sound/Spelling(s) Reviewed: /r/ spelled *wr, r;* /oo/ spelled *oo (took), ew, oo (moon);* /ū/ spelled *u;* /v/ spelled *v,* /ur/ spelled *ur,* /ō/ spelled *o_e, ow,* /ā/ spelled *a_e, ay;* /air/ spelled *air,* /z/ spelled *s,* /or/ spelled *or,* /er/ spelled *er,* /ē/ spelled *e, ea, ee;* /ī/ spelled *i_e, ie, igh;* /ū/ spelled *u;* /k/ spelled *k, ck;* /g/ spelled *g,* /w/ spelled *w_,* /sh/ spelled *sh,* /h/ spelled *h,* /b/ spelled *b,* /n/ spelled *n,* /ŭ/ spelled *u,* /ŏ/ spelled *o,* /p/ spelled *p,* /l/ spelled *l, ll;* /th/ (voiced) spelled *th,* /ĭ/ spelled *i,* /f/ spelled *f,* /ĕ/ spelled *e,* /d/ spelled *d,* /m/ spelled *m,* /a/ spelled *a,* /s/ spelled *s, ce;* /t/ spelled *t*

High-Frequency Words Reviewed: does, enough, taught, would, was, were, the, be, and, a, to, things, now, what, he, we, do, I, off, down, for

Credits

2 RSBPhoto/Alamy; **3** tom carter/Alamy; **4** Rob Goldman/ Photographer's Choice RF/Getty Images; **5** ©ThinkStock/ SuperStock; **6** ©M Stock/Alamy; **7** ©NPS photo; **8** Ingram Publishing/SuperStock; **9** lucato/Getty Images; **10** Olezzo/ iStock/Getty Images Plus/Getty Images; **11** Eclipse Studios/ McGraw-Hill Education; **12** ©D. Hurst/Alamy; **13** Paula Sierra/ Moment/Getty Images; **14** Lorraine Boogich/iStock/Getty Images Plus/Getty Images; **15** ilbusca/iStock/Getty Images Plus/Getty Images; **16** Sveti/iStock/Getty Images Plus/Getty Images; **17** Comstock Images/Alamy; **18** Ingram Publishing; **19** NASA; **20** Anikakodydkova/iStock/Getty Images Plus/ Getty Images; **21** Ingram Publishing/SuperStock; **22** Galina Barskaya/iStock/Getty Images Plus/Getty Images; **23** tirc83/ iStock/Getty Images Plus/Getty Images; **24** Christopher Futcher/E+/Getty Images; **25** yairleibo/iStock/Getty Images Plus/Getty Images; **26** Nancy Rose/Moment Open/Getty Images; **27** MCS 1st Class Matthew M. Bradley/US Navy/DoD; **28** Michael Krinke/iStock/Getty Images Plus/Getty Images; **29** (l)©Hero/Corbis/Glow Images, (r)karelnoppe/Getty Images; **30** Daniel Stone/National Cancer Institute (NCI); **31** Scott Harms/Getty Images; **32** Brett Hillyard/iStock/Getty Images Plus/Getty Images; **33** julos/iStock/Getty Images Plus/ Getty Images; **34** 4774344sean/iStock/Getty Images Plus/ Getty Images; **35 36** McGraw-Hill Education; **37** Design Pics/ Ben Welsh; **38** Jody Menard/Getty Images; **39** U.S. Fish & Wildlife Service/Steve Hillebrand; **40** Nikreates/Alamy; **41** Deb Perry/Getty Images; **43** Ingram Publishing; **45** Ewen Charlton/Getty Images; **46** Don Tremain/Getty Images; **49** rotofrank/iStock/Getty Images Plus/Getty Images; **51** Ingram Publishing/SuperStock; **52** Gregory Costanzo/ Digital Vision/Getty Images; **54** Yury Zap/iStock/Getty Images Plus/Getty Images; **56** Zoonar GmbH/Edith Albuschat/Alamy; **58** ©Ingram Publishing/Alamy; **60** Copyright © Foodcollection; **63** Michael Krinke/Getty Images; **64** ©Image Source, all rights reserved.; **67** (inset)National Archives and Records Administration [NWDNS-127-N-A374394], (bkgd) John Lund/Tiffany Schoepp/Blend Images LLC; **68** Steven P. Lynch; **71** Lorado/E+/Getty Images; **73** James Callaghan/ Alamy; **75** Don Nichols/E+/Getty Images; **77** abadonian/Getty Images; **78** Silvrshootr/iStock/Getty Images Plus/Getty Images; **81** Steven P. Lynch; **82** cherezoff/iStock/Getty Images Plus/Getty Images; **85** CoyStClair/iStock/Getty Images Plus/Getty Images; **87** ©Doug Sherman/Geofile; **89** Brand X/SuperStock; **91** theJIPEN/iStock/Getty Images Plus/Getty Images; **93** Kelly Pollak/iStock/Getty Images Plus/ Getty Images; **94** Anna Dyudina/Hemera/Getty Images Plus/ Getty Images; **96** U.S. Fish & Wildlife Service/Richard Stark; **99** Lissa Harrison; **101** Fuse/Getty Images; **103** Richard Hutchings/McGraw-Hill Education; **104** Alan Sealls/ WeatherVideoHD.TV; **107** David Robinson/Getty Images; **108** ©Steve Hamblin/Alamy; **110** Images-USA/Alamy; **113** Alastair Pollock Photography/Getty Images; **114** Ken Karp/ McGraw-Hill Education; **117** irin717/iStock/Getty Images Plus/ Getty Images; **119** Pixtal/AGE Fotostock; **121** ©U. S. Fish and Wildlife Service/William Troyer photographer; **123** ©Image Source, all rights reserved.; **124** Image Source/Getty Images; **126** Design Pics/Keith Levit; **129** Yale University Art Gallery; **131** Erica Simone Leeds; **133** Doug88888/Getty Images; **135** ©Michael S. Yamashita/Corbis; **137** Photographed by Lee Leng Kiong (Singapore)/Moment/Getty Images; **138** Bear Dancer Studios/Mark Dierker; **141** Doxieone Photography/ Moment Open/Getty Images; **142** Alan SCHEIN/Alamy; **144** Purestock/SuperStock; **147** Jupiterimages; **149** skiserge1/ iStock/Getty Images Plus/Getty Images; **151** LowellRichards/ iStock/Getty Images Plus/Getty Images; **152** Glow Images; **155** Ingram Publishing/SuperStock; **156** Tim Pannell/Fuse/ Getty Images; **158** ©Image Source/PunchStock; **161** Ruben Moreno Montoliu/Moment/Getty Images; **163** Terry Alexander/iStock/Getty Images Plus/Getty Images; **165** Dan Borsum, NOAA/NWS/WR/WFO/Billings Montana/Department of Commerce; **167** Berenika Lychak/iStock/Getty Images Plus/Getty Images; **168** U.S. Fish & Wildlife Service; **171** Eric Pearle/Stockbyte/Getty Images; **173** Image Created by James van den Broek/Moment Open/Getty Images; **175** Niall McDiarmid/Alamy; **177** Kirk Patrick, USDA Natural Resources Conservation Service; **179** McGraw-Hill Education; **180** Photo by R.B. Colton, USGS; **183** ©IT Stock Free; **185** Foto_by_M/ iStock/Getty Images Plus/Getty Images; **187** NPS Photo; **188** Design Pics/Alan Marsh; **191** Digital Vision/Punchstock; **193** 4774344sean/iStock/Getty Images Plus/Getty Images; **194** Radius Images/Getty Images Plus/Getty Images; **197** NOAA Photo Library, NOAA Central Library; OAR/ERL/ National Severe Storms Laboratory (NSSL); **199** ©William Leaman/Alamy; **200** Library of Congress Prints and Photographs Division [LC-USZ62-112792]; **202** Petrea Alexandru/E+/Getty Images; **205** ©Brand X Pictures/ Punchstock; **207** U.S. Air Force photo; **208** Library of Congress Prints & Photographs Division [LC-DIG-pppprs-00626].